# ACTION-GETTING RESUMES
## FOR TODAY'S JOBS

Gary Turbak

AN ARCO BOOK
PUBLISHED BY PRENTICE HALL PRESS
NEW YORK, NY 10023

First Edition

An Arco Book
Published by Prentice Hall Press
A Division of Simon & Schuster, Inc.
Gulf+Western Building
One Gulf+Western Plaza
New York, NY 10023

PRENTICE HALL PRESS is a trademark of
Simon & Schuster, Inc.

Manufactured in the United States of America

3   4   5   6   7   8   9   10

**Library of Congress Cataloging in Publication Data**

Turbak, Gary.
  Action-getting resumes for today's jobs.
  Includes index.
  1. Résumés (Employment) I. Title.
HF5383.T87   1983        650.1'4        83-3876
ISBN 0-668-05706-8 (Reference Text)
ISBN 0-668-05711-4 (Paper Edition)

To Hazel Benn, a connoisseur of the language.

# CONTENTS

1. **RESUME BASICS** ......................................................... 1
   Just What Is a Resume? ................................................. 1
   When and How to Use Your Resume ................................... 3
   Compiling the Information .............................................. 4
   Should You Write Your Own Resume? ................................ 4
   What Should NOT Go In Your Resume .............................. 5
   The Importance of Dates ............................................... 6
   Brevity Is Bliss ........................................................... 6

2. **RESUME LANGUAGE** .................................................... 7
   Language Techniques that Work Best ................................. 8
   Verbs with Verve ........................................................ 11
   Passive and Active Voice .............................................. 15
   Keep It Simple ........................................................... 15
   Grammar and Punctuation ............................................ 16
   Abbreviations ............................................................ 16
   The Editorial Red Pencil ............................................. 17
   From "Pride and Joy" to Bureaucratese ........................... 19

3. **BUILDING YOUR RESUME** ............................................ 20
   Name ...................................................................... 20
   Address ................................................................... 20
   Telephone Number ..................................................... 21
   Suggested Entries for Chronological Resumes .................... 22
   Employment History .................................................... 22
   Education ................................................................. 24
   Employment Objective ................................................. 26
   Resume Capsule ......................................................... 27
   Military ................................................................... 27
   Affiliations and Memberships ........................................ 28
   Publications .............................................................. 29
   Personal Information ................................................... 30
   Certifications ............................................................ 32
   General .................................................................... 32
   References ................................................................ 33

4. **CHOOSING A RESUME FORMAT** .................................... 34
   Chronological Resume .................................................. 34
   Functional Resume ..................................................... 37
   Creative Resume ........................................................ 39
   Make It Pretty ........................................................... 41

**5.  THE COVER LETTER** ........................................................ 43

    Conform to the Norm in Form ............................................. 44

    Contending with Content ................................................... 45

    Generally Speaking ........................................................ 48

    Other Kinds of Letters .................................................... 49

    Presentation and Design .................................................. 49

    Sample Letters ........................................................... 50

**6.  60 SAMPLE RESUMES** (See **Resume Index** on page vi) .............. 62

**7.  THE INTERVIEW** ............................................................ 155

    The Medium Is the Message ............................................... 155

    Kinds of Interviews ...................................................... 155

    Preparation .............................................................. 156

    Practice ................................................................. 157

    Asking the Asker ......................................................... 158

    Get There on Time ....................................................... 159

    You Can't Take It With You ............................................. 160

    Looking Like a Winner ................................................... 160

    Talking Without Words ................................................... 161

    Interview Etiquette ...................................................... 162

    Getting Your Message Across ............................................. 163

    Three Tough Questions ................................................... 164

    Getting Ready to Do It Again ............................................ 166

# RESUME INDEX

| OCCUPATION | PAGE | FORMAT |
|---|---|---|
| Insurance Agent | 63 | Chronological |
| Librarian | 65 | Chronological |
| Retailer (photo) | 67 | Chronological |
| Manager (industry) | 69 | Chronological |
| Travel Agent | 71 | Chronological |
| School Principal | 72 | Chronological |
| Police Officer | 73 | Chronological |
| Tax Preparer | 74 | Chron./Functional |
| Dental Assistant | 75 | Chronological |
| Production Worker | 76 | Chronological |
| Biologist | 77 | Chronological |
| Automotive Mechanic | 79 | Chronological |
| Construction Worker | 81 | Chronological |
| Salesperson | 82 | Chronological |
| Businessperson | 84 | Chronological |
| Market Researcher | 86 | Chronological |
| Manager (auto) | 88 | Chronological |
| Business Administrator | 90 | Chronological |
| Manager/Salesperson | 92 | Chronological |
| Hospital Director | 94 | Chronological |
| Flight Attendant | 96 | Chronological |
| Construction Worker | 98 | Chronological |
| Retail Clerk | 99 | Chronological |
| Bank Teller | 100 | Chronological |
| Attorney | 101 | Chronological |
| Draftsman | 103 | Chronological |
| Forester | 104 | Chronological |
| Medical Technologist | 106 | Chronological |
| Electrician | 108 | Chronological |
| Carpenter | 110 | Chronological |
| Manager (business) | 111 | Chronological |
| Accountant | 113 | Chronological |
| Teacher | 115 | Chronological |
| Lifeguard | 117 | Chronological |
| Nurse | 118 | Chronological |
| Salesperson | 120 | Chronological |
| Administrator | 121 | Chronological |
| Geologist | 122 | Chronological |
| Journalist | 124 | Chronological |
| Accountant | 126 | Functional |
| Lobbyist | 127 | Functional |
| Custodian | 128 | Functional |
| Manager (business) | 129 | Functional |

# RESUME INDEX

| OCCUPATION | PAGE | FORMAT |
|---|---|---|
| Laborer | 130 | Functional |
| Police Officer | 131 | Functional |
| Pharmacist | 133 | Functional |
| Optician | 135 | Functional |
| Varied Background—<br>Business/Insurance/<br>Construction | 136 | Functional |
| Timber Broker | 137 | Functional |
| Manager/Salesperson | 138 | Functional |
| Waitress | 140 | Functional |
| Secretary | 141 | Functional |
| Guide | 142 | Functional |
| Accountant/Manager | 143 | Functional |
| Photographer | 145 | Functional |
| Retail Salesperson | 147 | Chronological |
| Manager (government) | 149 | Functional |
| Teacher | 151 | Functional |
| Advertising Agent | 153 | Creative |
| Disk Jockey | 154 | Creative |

# Chapter 1

# RESUME BASICS

So, you need a resume. You're not alone. Every year, millions of people enter the work force or change employment. Most of these job seekers use the resume as the basic tool in their search for that perfect job. Job hunting with an effective resume in hand should be as standard a practice as wearing clean clothes to an interview. Attempting to land a new job—especially a better paying one—without a forceful, descriptive resume is like trying to catch a fish without a hook on the end of your line. It's possible, but the odds are against you.

## Just What Is a Resume?

"Resume" is a French word that means "summary." It is pronounced REZ OO MA. Your resume is, in essence, a summary of you. It's a condensation of your educational background, work history, skills, abilities, and other attributes. Technically, the word "resume" should be written with an accent mark over each "e" (like this: résumé), but it appears throughout this book without the marks, and you needn't worry about them either.

Your resume will serve you by conserving your valuable time. When applying for several jobs, all you need do is write a brief, personalized letter to each employer and enclose a pre-printed copy of your resume. If you had to explain your skills, abilities, and background in detail in each letter, job hunting would be a slow and tedious task. In an interview, where every precious second counts, you need not waste time answering basic questions about your past because your trusty resume has already answered them for you.

And a resume is one of the easiest documents in the world to update. In a few years, when you have a new job experience to include, you simply add a brief section to your current resume and retype. This will also save you time.

Above all else, your resume will function as an advertisement—an advertisement of what you have to offer an employer. Almost nothing is sold these days without the proper advertising, and your skills are no exception. But don't let this make you think of yourself as little more than a can of beer or a bar of soap. Instead, picture yourself as the latest model imported sportscar in search of the perfect buyer. The competition for good jobs is keen, and the people who do the best job of selling themselves are the ones who end up on an employer's payroll.

It used to be that blue collar, unskilled, and very young workers thought they did not need a resume. Resumes, the thinking went, were for executives, professionals, and people with complex employment histories. While that may have been true once, it certainly isn't today. If you are interested in a specific job, you can be certain that other people are too. That means you're going to have competition, and one way to get ahead of the competition is to present a high quality resume to a prospective employer. **FOR ANY OCCUPATION**, whether you're a teacher, carpenter, farm hand, junior executive, store clerk, nurse, stock broker, or jelly bean polisher, you are more likely to land a good job when you have a quality resume in your possession.

1

Your resume must be a plea that says "Hire Me!" just as obviously as your supermarket's flyer says "Buy Chicken." Effective advertisements—the ones that attract buyers—consistently have three traits in common: (1) they are brief; (2) the message comes across loud and clear; (3) they are pleasing to look at. They don't bombard readers with incidental, unimportant information. There's no doubt about what they're trying to say. And you don't have to squint or shield your eyes to read them.

Let's consider for a moment two kinds of advertisements we've all seen in newspapers. Both appear as full-page ads. The first is a pitch to buy a particular brand of cigarettes. The second is an ad for a new diet book that's "guaranteed" to help you shed extra pounds.

The cigarette ad features a cowboy on a horse, a smiling bathing beauty, or some other wholesome and healthy-looking person. There aren't many words in the ad (perhaps as few as 25) and the size of the type is varied. The printed message is easy to read. Much of the full page is blank space with the picture and words attractively laid out. In two or three seconds, you the reader get the message. If you're in the market for a new brand of cigarette, there's a good chance you'll do exactly as the cigarette maker asks. The ad is concise; the message is clear; the page is pleasing to look at.

Now the diet ad. Things are different here. Across the top of the page is a headline of some sort. Perhaps it says "New Diet Plan Works Wonders." Most of the rest of the page is filled with tightly fitted copy in small type. There are perhaps 1,500 words here. In the center of the page may be a slightly blurry photograph of a man in a white frock. Somewhere near the bottom of the page may be a small "clip and mail" blank with cramped lines for your name and address. This ad is confusing. It looks somewhat like a newspaper story, but it isn't. The page, heavy with type, looks tedious. There's too much message here, and most readers won't read all of this ad.

So it is with resumes. An effective resume, one that will help you land a job, must be brief, clear, and appealing. It must be the best possible advertisement for the product you're selling—yourself.

What you must *NOT* do, then, is consider the preparation of your resume to be a perfunctory task that is done only to satisfy a personnel director in some large office. Simply getting the facts down on paper usually is not enough. You must write a resume that will hold a reader's attention through to the end and will leave that person with a keen awareness of what you can do for him/her. This book can help you accomplish that important task.

In practical terms, your resume will have a single, all-important purpose: To entice an employer into granting you a job interview. After the interview, your resume may stay with the employer as a tangible reminder of your skills, but its job has already been done. The impression you make in an interview will likely carry more weight than your resume. Once you sit down in that chair for your interview, your resume has largely served its purpose.

From the employer's point of view, resumes are indispensable too. They provide him/her with a quick and easy way to screen out candidates who probably aren't right for the job. If a firm had to interview each applicant to find out which few were the best qualified, a lot of valuable time would be wasted. So employers are always on the lookout for resumes that sparkle and shine and clearly tell them what they need to know. In this sense, the resume you put in an employer's hands can determine your future.

# When and How to Use Your Resume

Try to think of your resume as an expanded version of that standard business tool, the calling card. No sales representative would think of meeting people without a supply of business cards on hand, and you should be prepared to use your resume the same way. Resumes can't be carried in pocket or purse, of course, but your attitude about disseminating them should be the same. Be prepared to give your resume to anyone you think may be interested in buying what you have to sell: your skills and abilities.

One place where resumes are actively solicited by employers is in newspaper want ads. "Send letter of application and resume," the ad may say. This is exactly what you should do. (Cover letters are discussed in Chapter 5 of this book.) This type of ad can generate hundreds of applications, so a top-notch resume is really crucial here.

Job openings advertised in college placement bureaus and at government offices also are best pursued with a resume.

When you make the rounds of state and local employment services, take a supply of resumes with you. Leave one at each stop. Anywhere anyone is keeping an employment file on you, there also should be a copy of your current resume. Don't be shy about handing them out.

If you are an aggressive job seeker and are making cold calls (simply knocking on employers' doors to see if any openings exist), ask at each business if you may leave a resume there. Even if there are no openings now, one may occur next week, and you'll want your resume to be on file. Every job inquiry you make through the mail should contain a copy of your resume.

Employers of all sorts expect applicants to supply resumes. Even if you fill out a detailed application form, leave a resume too. Even if the employer doesn't request a resume, leave one with him/her. The firm will be impressed by the seriousness with which you're approaching your search for a new job.

Another market for your resume is commercial employment agencies. Even medium-sized cities have several of these. You may want to register and leave your resume with one or more of them (after you thoroughly understand what it will cost you if that firm eventually finds a job for you). But even if you don't want to register right now, the employment counselor may be willing to keep a copy of your resume nearby and call you when a promising job opening turns up.

Finally, you may want to "broadcast" your resume to potential employers. A phone book's yellow pages or city directory can provide you with names and addresses of all potential employers in your field. Eager-beaver job hunters will send a letter and resume to each of these employers just in case an unadvertised opening exists.

The rule, again, is this: *Distribute your resume anywhere and everywhere an opportunity for employment (or future employment) exists*. If you think it will help your chances of getting a job, tack a copy of your resume to the bulletin board in your neighborhood laundromat. In this case, it might be wise to omit your home telephone number and give a post office box as a forwarding address. It's truly counterproductive to create a good resume and then hoard the copies as if they were shares of Xerox stock. Get the word about yourself into the hands of the people who do the hiring.

And always be sure to keep a list of firms to which you've sent a resume. In the hubbub of job hunting, it's easy to apply twice to the same company. Doing that may make you appear to be a bit disorganized.

# Compiling the Information

Fortunately, gathering the necessary information for your resume is an easy chore. Some employment counselors and resume books suggest that you formally fill out a detailed "Personal Inventory Form" before attempting to write your resume. Usually, this is not necessary. Just about every piece of information you'll need for your resume is already on call in your head, and it'll save you time if you commit it to paper directly in resume format instead of making extensive preliminary lists.

First, study this book so you'll have a good solid knowledge of what resumes should look and sound like. Then take a sheet of paper and begin to write the first draft of your resume in the format you've chosen. You'll need a rewrite or two, but this is the fastest way to put an excellent resume together.

You may, however, need to look up in personal records the exact dates of previous employment, the spelling of a former employer's name, your college grade point average, and other specific details out of your past. The least time-consuming way to do this is simply to have all your records handy and ferret out the information as it is needed for your resume.

# Should You Write Your Own Resume?

In a word, yes. There are professional writers in nearly every city who, for a fee of $25 to $100, will be happy to interview you and write your resume for you. They may even do a very good job of it. I have written scores of resumes for job seekers, and I certainly think I've given them excellent documents with which to approach the job market. In fact, many of my clients have called to let me know that the resume I wrote helped them get a job. But most of my resume clients (a) have not been concerned with how much their resume costs them, (b) have needed a high-quality resume in a big hurry, and/or (c) have had very little confidence in their ability to put ideas down on paper.

But if you don't want your resume to cost any more than necessary, if you have a couple hours or so to devote to its creation, and if you're on reasonably good terms with the English language, you can easily write your own resume. You obviously are interested in writing your own resume, or you wouldn't have this book in your hands right now. Rest assured, you CAN produce your own professional resume with very little difficulty.

By writing the resume yourself, you can be sure that it is a complete and accurate representation of your backgound and abilities. It will be a unique document. Some professional resume writers have a library of stock paragraphs which they use again and again to describe certain jobs. The result is that many of their clients' resumes begin to look alike, even down to word-for-word explanations of past job responsibilities. Employers often can spot these resume-factory documents and will look more favorably upon your self-written resume. A well-written resume also is a good testimonial to your ability to organize your thoughts and put them down on paper—skills that are important in many jobs.

And, by learning to prepare your own resume, you'll be ready and able to update it a year or more from now. A resume is like a spouse: one good one is all you'll ever need. If you take the time now to prepare an effective resume, adding to it as years go by will be a simple chore.

# What Should NOT Go In Your Resume

Chapter 3 of this book will cover in detail the components of an effective resume. Many items are optional, and these will be discussed then. There are, however, a few items that sometimes tend to creep into resumes when they really should not be there. Perhaps a long time ago they were correctly included, but current practice dictates that they be omitted from resumes in the 1980s. They are:

*Salary requirements.* Do not state on your resume that you must be offered a salary of $40,000 (or whatever) before you'll come to work for a firm. Don't say so even if it's true. Here's the reason: If the company is willing to pay a salary of $45,000 and you request only $40,000, you have just robbed yourself of $5,000. If the firm has in mind a top salary of $38,500, you likely will not be considered for the job, even though you're only $1,500 per year apart. Either way, you lose. A few employment applications still ask specifically for a job seeker's salary needs. You can respond by stating your salary requirements in words, not numbers. You can, for example, ask for pay "commensurate with training and abilities," "based on experience," "in line with assigned responsibilities," or "in mid-range with the possibility of early increases for outstanding performance." If possible, though, avoid all mention of salary in your resume. Save that juicy topic for the interview.

*Reasons for leaving previous jobs.* Usually, any attempt to explain why you quit past jobs fails because of the truncated format of the resume. There simply isn't room in a resume to do justice to the often complicated reasons for leaving a job. Trying to explain why you left will only draw unnecessary attention to the matter. If the prospective employer is concerned about your previous moves, he/she will bring it up during the interview.

*Names of references.* Names, addresses, and phone numbers of people you intend to use as references should never appear on your resume. A prospective employer won't care what other people think about you until after he/she interviews you. Listing references on your resume, then, is putting the plow before the mule. You may, of course, make some general statement, such as: "References Available Upon Request."

*Names of spouse and/or children.* You are the only person an employer is interested in. No one cares to know who your husband, wife, or children are, so don't put their names on your resume. However, you may, in the "Personal" section of your resume, mention your marital status and the number of children you have if you think it will be to your advantage to do so.

*A photograph.* Unless you're applying for a job as a model in TV toothpaste commercials, no one cares what you look like. It is generally considered to be in poor taste to attach a photo of yourself (or of anyone else, for that matter) to your resume. If you're really one of the beautiful people, that fact will become quite apparent when you're interviewed. And by attaching a photo you always run the risk that the employer may not like the shape of your nose or the way you comb your hair. Legally, you cannot be discriminated against on such a cosmetic basis, but there's a chance a resume reader may subconsciously be turned off by your appearance.

*Anything negative.* A resume is a place for you to proclaim your talents, not confess your shortcomings. There's no need to mention a divorce, handicap, health problem, or other factors that may detract from your strong points. These topics are important, but they are better discussed in a cover letter or during an interview.

# The Importance of Dates

When you begin to prepare your resume, one factor you must keep in mind is how you plan to handle dates—the dates of employment, education, etc. In some cases, a resume will have to account for all time since completion of grammar school. This is not always done in great detail, but it's good to let employers know that you've been engaged in productive activities through the years.

For most people this is not a problem. They simply work backward from the present, explaining what they did when. But if you have spent time in prison, have been unemployed for a long period, or have otherwise been outside of what society considers its productive mainstream, you may want to camouflage that fact a bit (not hide it, just make it less prominent). Handling dates will be discussed in greater detail in Chapter 4, so for now just begin thinking about how an employer might react to a chronological breakdown of your past.

# Brevity Is Bliss

The cardinal rule in writing your resume is: KEEP IT SHORT. Many more resumes fail because they're too wordy than because they're too brief. Employers, especially those in larger firms, sometimes have to sort through hundreds (or even thousands) of resumes for each position they fill. Some busy resume readers spend an average of only 30 seconds on each resume. Long resumes tend to put them to sleep. What they want to see are crisp, tightly written, BRIEF resumes. Remember, a resume is a SUMMARY. It is supposed to be short. It should be a proverb, not a novel.

How much is too much? Acceptable resume length varies with the age and experience of its owner, and a resume can be as long as it needs to be. Good guidelines, however, are these: One page is great. Two pages are okay if you have been busy for a few years. Three pages are probably too many, unless you're a senior executive type with decades of top-level management experience to your credit. Of course, I'm speaking here of formatted resume pages—that is, the resume in its final form. A happy medium that most people can shoot for is about one and a half pages. (But there is absolutely nothing wrong with a one-page resume.) One or two pages seems like precious little space on which to effectively summarize your life history, but it can be done. The people who get the interviews—and, hence, the jobs—are the people who do it best. This book will help you become one of them.

# Chapter 2

# RESUME LANGUAGE

Resumes are unique documents. They are written in the kind of verbal short-hand that sets English teachers to pulling their hair and gnashing their teeth. Resume language is different because a great deal must be said in very little space. In that sense, the use of English in resumes is most closely akin to the language used in newspaper want ads (which shouldn't be surprising, because your resume is really one big advertisement). Anyway, the terse style and short, incomplete sentences of the *Independent Courier's* want ads are similar to the kind of language you'll be creating in your resume. Good resume writing is about as closely related to high school themes and college papers as are radishes to chickens.

Your resume language will break many of the rules drilled into your head throughout junior high school. In resumes, complete sentences often are not necessary. Frequently, the subject of a sentence will be missing, just like the horseman's head in *The Legend of Sleepy Hollow*. Sentences will invariably be short and choppy. Entire words may be capitalized to stress their importance. Paragraphs, as such, will be nonexistent. Adjectives and adverbs will be held to a minimum. In short, if you wrote anything else the way you're going to write your resume, you'd be considered a failure. But because acceptable resume style has evolved the way it has, you'll be a success, and probably on your way to that first important interview.

Before we begin discussing specifics, let's take a general look at two different ways to present some information. First:

> My original duties with the company included driving and loading trucks. Later I was promoted to the dispatch office where I became responsible for scheduling the arrivals and departures of up to 25 vehicles per day. Presently, I supervise all activities in the firm's shipping department. This means I am fully responsible for approximately 50 employees.

This piece of writing is very informative and well constructed. But it is much too wordy for a resume. Try this version for size:

> Began as driver/loader. Later advanced to dispatch office. Scheduled arrivals and departures for 25 vehicles daily. Earned promotion to head of shipping department. Presently supervise 50 employees.

The first example contains 56 words and the second 28. A victory for brevity! This is the language of the resume. Here's another example, this time from the resume of a secretary:

> I am primarily responsible for maintaining the files, typing, writing letters, receiving customers, and doing some light bookkeep-

ing. My other duties include taking orders over the phone and frequently answering customers' questions. Sometimes I resolve complaints. I also compute the payroll.

And the slimmed down version:

> Maintain files, conduct correspondence, type, receive customers, and do light bookkeeping. Also take phone orders and handle customer questions and complaints.

Again, all the essential information remains on the second version, but the fat has been trimmed away. One credo to follow in writing your resume is: GET RID OF THE FAT.

Time is precious. You may spend a few hours preparing and writing your resume, but it will be read in a flash. Personnel directors and other hirers and firers don't curl up in front of an evening fire with a glass of wine and a stack of good resumes. They skim them in a busy office setting that puts countless demands on their time. To get your sales pitch across to them, you must deliver as much information as you can in as little space as possible. If their interest is not piqued in the half minute or so they initially devote to each resume, the document goes in the circular file and your job chances go out the window. NEVER USE THREE WORDS WHEN TWO WILL DO.

# Language Techniques that Work Best

Now, let's begin discussing the specific language techniques that will help you say the most in the least space. To do this, we'll have to temporarily revert to using that junior high school English jargon. Remember pronouns? Pronouns are the words that take the place of nouns in a sentence. He, she, it, they, my, their, our, I, and him are all pronouns. There are lots more too. Relax. The only pronouns we're going to be concerned with here are I, he/she, my, and his/her.

In resumes, pronouns get in the way. Long ago, someone decided that a resume sprinkled with "I," "me," and "my" looked and sounded pompous, redundant, and clumsy. That person was right, and resumes ever since have banished these pronouns. No self-respecting resume should ever contain such lines as these:

> Most of my experience has been in cost accounting.

> or

> I have had six years of training on the Model IT–200.

> or

> The firm's "Employee of the Year" award was given to me three years in a row.

In writing your resume, steer clear of the "my," "I," and "me" that brand the above lines with the obvious mark of the unprofessional writer.

There are several good reasons for the omission of the personal pronouns. First, these words, tiny though they may be, take up space, and space is at a premium in a resume. Every non-essential word that's eliminated will make room for another more important one.

Second, every resume reader knows that the document is relating the history of the person whose name appears at the top of the page. It is unnecessary for you to be constantly reminding the reader that the resume is proclaiming your virtues. Personal pronouns are superfluous.

More important, however, the elimination of these personal pronouns will allow you to feel more comfortable in saying grand and glorious things about yourself. Most of us are blest with at least a modicum of modesty, and it's often difficult to blow our own horns as loudly as they need to be tooted. With the pronouns gone, you're more likely to say more good things about yourself. It just seems less pompous and more like an objective evaluation if the pronouns are eliminated. Consider these three resume sentences:

I have outstanding mathematical abilities.

and

My mathematical abilities are outstanding.

and

Outstanding mathematical abilities.

The third example not only takes up less space, but it seems to be rendering an objective opinion about the resume owner's math capabilities. Everyone knows WHO has the math abilities. By eliminating the pronouns, space is saved and no trace of arrogance peeks through. Strange as it may sound, you should strive to keep yourself (at least in pronoun form) out of your own resume.

But you must still be aware of the missing pronouns. The verb in the sentence must agree with the subject, even when the subject pronoun is not there. A sentence that would appear in the real world as "I slice kumquats" becomes "Slice kumquats" in a resume. The verb "slice" agrees with the missing subject pronoun "I." Another form of the verb—"slices"—does not agree with the subject "I" and would not be used if the missing pronoun were "I." If, however, the missing pronoun were "he," then the verb must be "slices."

If you're following all this, you're about to say that you don't see a problem here: I simply write the sentence as though the subject "I" were there, you say, and all is fine, right? The sentence:

I supervise 20 journeymen.

would then become

Supervise 20 journeymen.

You're absolutely correct—except that you have an option in writing your resume that can cause subject-verb disagreement if you're not careful. The option is this: You may write your resume as though the missing pronouns were "he" or "she" and not "I." Using "he" or "she" can make your resume sound as though it had been written by someone other than you. The advantage of doing it this way is that a further flavor of objectivity is lent to the document. Which version of these two examples, the "I" or the "He," seems more objective and believable? The first:

(I) Repeatedly create some of the nation's best radio commercials.

or

(He) Repeatedly creates some of the nation's best radio commercials.

And the second:

(I) Annually devise effective new methods of cost production.

or

(He) Annually devises effective new methods of cost production.

You should be able to see the difference, even though it is a subtle distinction. It's easier for many people to write good things about themselves if it appears that someone else did the writing. In most other forms of writing this might be frowned upon, but in your resume you do have this option.

The rub, of course, is that "I" and "he/she" sometimes take different forms of the verb. The distinction is slight but it is important, especially when *any* flaw in the resume may reduce your chances of getting an interview.

Which pronoun you use (*in absentia*, of course) matters most when you are dealing with your present employment or educational status and are therefore using present tense verbs. In the past tense, the verb forms are the same regardless of the pronoun you're using. For example, in the present tense, the verbs change depending upon which pronoun you're using:

(I) Recruit donors, match blood types, and draw blood.

but

(He) Recruits donors, matches blood types, and draws blood.

In the past tense, however, the difference between verb forms disappears, and you no longer need to worry about which pronoun you have in mind. For example:

(I) Recruited donors, matched blood types, and drew blood.

and

(He) Recruited donors, matched blood types, and drew blood.

In addition to using the present tense to describe your current employment, you may want to use it as well in stating an employment objective, summarizing, presenting general information, and in other special sections. In describing all former employment and education, you'll use past tense.

Which approach should you use, the "he/she" or the "I"? It doesn't really matter. Both are acceptable. The important thing is to be aware that two forms exist and to stick with one form throughout your resume. The only mistake you can make is to switch back and forth between the two within your resume. Most people seem to be more comfortable writing about themselves in first person (the "I" form).

If all this bustle about pronouns and verb tense seems to be much ado about nothing, keep in mind that your resume probably will be the most exacting document you will ever write. It must be written precisely. Any error in your resume reflects negatively on you.

Don't let this jargon overwhelm you. If "tense" to you is what happens when you're asked to speak in front of a group of people, fear not. Like many other straightforward actions, the construction of your resume appears much more difficult in description than it is in practice. Why, it would take six typewritten pages to fully explain how to tie shoelaces, and even then most of us would get it wrong. What shoe tiers and resume writers both need are good illustrations. In Chapter 6 of this book you'll find numerous sample resumes. They'll provide quick illustration of the not-really-very-complicated pronoun requirements of a good resume. Read several of them, and you'll begin to get a feel for resume language.

# Verbs with Verve

You can be technically correct in your use of resume language without being particularly effective. Some kinds of words ARE more important than others, and it'll pay for you to know which ones pack a wallop. Here's a ranking of the importance the major parts of speech usually play in a resume: (1) Verbs, (2) Nouns and Pronouns, (3) Adverbs, and (4) Adjectives.

Don't worry, we're not going to turn this book into a text for Parts of Speech 101, but, after all, language is what your resume is all about. Now, let's quickly dispense with three of the aforementioned kinds of words and concentrate on the most important species.

*Adjectives* should be used in your resume only under duress. They are the words—small, large, blue, pretty, delicious, good, and so forth—that describe people or things. Adjectives are to a good resume as candles are to the modern home: ornamental nearly all of the time. Your resume is essentially a document that tells of the actions (work) you have done or are capable of doing. Adjectives just aren't up to the task of saying much about you that a prospective employer is interested in knowing. One exception may be in a resume's "General" section, where you might wish to describe yourself as a "loyal, dedicated, honest, ambitious employee." Usually, though, strings of adjectives such as this don't work well in resumes. Employers want to hear the specifics of what you can do, not glowing generalities. Most of the time, a concept is more forceful when expressed with adverbs than with adjectives. (We'll compare the two in a moment.) A list of adjectives you may wish to consider is in Chapter 5.

*Adverbs* are the words that usually tell HOW something was done. You may remember that most of them end with "ly." Precisely, effectively, wisely, slowly, and quickly are all adverbs. Your use of adverbs in your resume will probably be limited to a very few inserted carefully (there's another one) into the proper spot. Guard against their overuse. Every verb does not need an adverb. In this resume sentence

> Quickly earned promotion to department manager

"quickly" tells a prospective employer that your promotion came after a relatively short time on the job. The adverb serves a purpose here. However, in this sentence

> Learned to install radios quickly on auto assembly line

"quickly" doesn't add much. How else would you install things on an assembly line? At a leisurely pace? Make sure the adverb you're using serves a specific purpose.

Now, let's compare adjectives and adverbs. Many words are available for your use in both forms: slow and slowly, quick and quickly, careful and carefully, and so on. Here's the choice with which you may be faced. Do you say in your resume

> Was an effective manager of 25 restaurant employees.

> or

> Effectively managed 25 restaurant employees.

And how about this pair of possibilities:

> As brain surgeon, learned to do precise work.

> or

> As brain surgeon, learned to work precisely.

To most readers, the adverb form (the second in both of these examples) sounds better and delivers a stronger message. This may not always be the case, but in writing your resume you should continually ask yourself if there might be a better way to say something. Often, that better way is with an adverb rather than an adjective.

*Nouns and pronouns*, of course, are necessary in all kinds of writing. Pronouns we've already talked about. Nouns are the names of the places, companies, equipment, products, people, positions, courses of study, and processes that make up your complete background. They are what they are, and we have relatively little to say about them. Often, they choose us; we do not choose them. The correct nouns will fall into place as you write your resume, and you don't need to worry much about them.

About the only precaution you should take is to avoid calling a spade a "single-operator, non-motorized entrenching tool." If you've worked as a janitor, call yourself a "janitor" (or the equally acceptable "custodian"). Don't try to pass yourself off as a "maintenance engineer." If you've been a "teacher's aide," don't say you were a "classroom facilitator." If you've seen duty as "lumberjack," don't claim to have been a "wood products supply specialist." Tell it like it is and you should encounter no problems with nouns.

This brings us to the *verbs*. They are the "workhorses" of the English language. They move the action, display the emotion, tote the barges, lift the bales, climb the mountains, and swim the seas.

Far and away, in every case, without exception, under all circumstances, VERBS ARE THE MOST IMPORTANT WORDS IN A RESUME. Verbs carry the message, give the resume force and body, and most accurately describe your strengths. Concentrate your writing skills on the verbs and you'll produce the best possible resume.

Verbs tell what you can do, and CAN DO is the name of the job hunting game. Let's look at these two examples from an auto mechanic's resume:

> Did tune-ups, brake work, and alignments. Was responsible for three other mechanics. Worked with customers in making appointments and with complaints. Used all modern auto shop equipment.

Here are the verbs from this entry (which is typical of the way many people tend to write their resumes): did, was, worked, and used. An impressive group? Absolutely not! These verbs lie there, half asleep, like so many cats in the afternoon sun. And fall asleep is what an employer or personnel director is likely to do when he/she reads such a bland resume. Here's the revision:

> Tuned engines, repaired brakes, and aligned front ends. Supervised three other mechanics. Scheduled customer appointments and resolved complaints. Operated all modern auto shop equipment.

Do these verbs sound better than the last ones: tuned, repaired, aligned, supervised, scheduled, resolved, and operated? Quite an improvement, I'd say! This entry now packs a punch. It's vibrant, alive, and informative. This resume sounds like it belongs to someone who's busy, productive, and multi-skilled. And this version is a few words *shorter* than the first.

Let's look at another example, this time from the resume of a manager of a neighborhood convenience store:

> Am responsible for all aspects of store management. Select employees and do ordering, pricing, inventory, advertising, stocking, and banking. Received company merit award three consecutive years.

Does this sound like a reasonable way to describe one's job? Perhaps. There's nothing TECHNICALLY wrong with this entry. All the essential information is there. But it doesn't stand up and shout "Here's what I can do!" It doesn't grab a prospective employer by the lapels and say "Hey, look at me." Here are the verbs from this entry: am, select, do, and received. Are these the kind of words you'd want representing you before an employer? Would you trust your future to lackluster words like these? Many people do just that when they really don't have to. With just a little extra thought you can add zest to your verbs. Here's a much more dynamic version of the last entry:

> Manage all aspects of store operation. Hire and fire employees. Order merchandise, calculate prices, inventory supplies, create advertising, stock shelves, and bank receipts. Earned company merit award three consecutive years.

Now the verbs here are: manage, hire, fire, order, calculate, inventory, stock, bank, and earned. You can see the difference, and so can the employers who'll be reading the resume you write.

Now, if you've been paying close attention, you've noticed a couple of similarities between the two entries we've just revised and improved. One of these is the elimination of any form of the word "responsible." Many a job seeker's first attempt at resume writing results in a construction like this:

> Responsibilities included filing reports, typing, preparing daily memorandums, and relieving the full-time receptionist during her lunch hour.

and this:

> Was responsible for keeping daily inventory, preparing employee attendance records, and recording vacation schedules for personnel.

Sometimes the word "duties" is used in a similar fashion ("Duties included . . ."). What these constructions do is make "include" or "was" the only verb in the sentence then trail a list of gerunds (a kind of noun derived from a verb) after that one weak verb. These sentences are as weak and flat as that can of soda you opened yesterday. Avoid this kind of listing if at all possible. Use strong, active verbs to tell about your abilities and experience. Make each verb stand on its own.

Another observation you may have made about the examples is that the revised versions frequently employed the same root words as the originals, but the form of the word had changed. "Did tune ups, brake work and alignments" became "Tuned engines, repaired brakes, and aligned front ends." In the other example, "do ordering, pricing, inventory, advertising, stocking, and banking" became "order merchandise, calculate prices, inventory supplies, create advertising, stock shelves, and bank receipts."

Unless it is absolutely unavoidable, never string a list of activities behind the weak verbs "do," "did," "capable of," "worked at," "experienced at," and other such constructions. Give each of your abilities its own verb.

Instead of saying:

> Capable of typing, filing, and taking dictation.

write

> Type, file, and take dictation.

You may have to add a word or two, but the increased effectiveness makes the change worthwhile.

There's no such thing as a complete list of the verbs you should use in your resume, but here are a few that can be effective. These are all listed in the present tense, but you are just as likely to use the past tense form. And, of course, each occupation has a repertoire of verbs all its own.

| | | |
|---|---|---|
| organize | achieve | accelerate |
| earn | create | support |
| manage | direct | adapt |
| supervise | hire and fire | structure |
| control | sell | analyze |
| build | advise | solve |
| revise | maintain | schedule |
| construct | write | approve |
| select | decide | assist |
| develop | teach | review |
| increase | administer | complete |

| | | |
|---|---|---|
| conceive | design | demonstrate |
| initiate | accomplish | eliminate |
| improve | handle | reorganize |
| operate | conduct | establish |
| plan | prepare | reinforce |
| produce | coordinate | evaluate |
| implement | perform | expand |
| reduce | recommend | program |
| propose | generate | launch |
| participate | originate | motivate |
| lecture | lead | influence |

# Passive and Active Voice

One linguistic construction you should try to avoid in your resume is an animal called passive voice. Whenever possible, use the species called active voice. The following paragraphs give a brief review of the difference between the two.

English sentences normally have a flow of action FROM a subject THROUGH a verb TO an object. The sentence "The iguana bit the turnip" is an example of this kind of writing. Via the verb "bit," the action flows from the iguana to the turnip. This is active voice. Use it whenever you can. This is the best possible way in the English language to express action.

Passive voice imparts the same meaning, but it does so in a clumsier, less powerful manner. "The turnip was bitten by the iguana" is passive voice. The flow of action is reversed, moving from the end of the sentence (where the iguana now lives) to the front. This is a decidedly weaker way to write.

Passive voice doesn't attempt to infiltrate resume writing all that often, but it can happen. The phrase "was promoted to manager," which is passive voice, takes the impetus for the action away from you and gives it to the person who did the promoting. It would be better for you to say "earned promotion to manager" or "became manager." This makes you, not some supervisor, responsible for the promotion. Likewise, the phrase "was given award for loyalty" should read "won award for loyalty." "Was graduated from Harvard" becomes "graduated from Harvard," and so on. Whenever possible, give yourself credit for the progress you've made.

Spotting passive voice in your resume writing can be difficult. The weak-kneed animal is even adept at slipping into the writing of professionals. Be on the lookout for sentences that, in their complete form, have the verb "was" and the word "by." In the examples above, the complete sentences would be: "I WAS promoted to manager BY the company owner." "I WAS given an award for loyalty BY the firm." "I WAS graduated from Harvard BY the board of regents." Don't get paranoid about the passive voice attacking your resume, but do be aware that it exists.

# Keep It Simple

Another thing you should not do in your resume is attempt to impress employers with lofty language and large words. We've already discussed inflated job descriptions, but there are other places in a resume where people like to pump in hot air. If you want to refer to money, use "salary," not "remuneration" (and, remember, it's not a good idea to mention the specific salary you'd like). You "attend" a college, not "matriculate" at it. You've had "varied," not "multifaceted" work experience. Don't use the word "deleterious" if "harmful" will do. Don't "render assistance to" if "help" will suffice. Don't "conceptualize" if "think of" means the same thing. (By the way, be wary of nearly all words ending in "ize," such as verbalize, finalize, visualize, theorize, and their many cousins.) Be continually asking yourself: Is there a shorter, simpler, better way to say it? If there is, use it.

# Grammar and Punctuation

Many of the set-in-stone rules of English grammar fall by the wayside when resumes are being written. Subjects (mostly in the form of the personal pronouns "I," "he," and "she") are left out of sentences. Sometimes the verbs are omitted. Occasionally, you may wish to type an important word all in capital letters or to underline it. A good general guideline is this: If the sentence gets the message across and is not offensive to the ear, it's okay. WARNING: If you are not accustomed to discerning subtle discrepancies in grammar, you may wish to have your resume proofread by a friend with a more sensitive ear. In most cases, though, you should be able to write an excellent resume without outside help. Consult the sample resumes in this book for ideas on how to handle various sections of your resume.

A few rules of grammar and punctuation remain unassailable even in a resume. The verb form MUST agree with the subject, even if the subject is only implied. (Refer to the discussion on pronouns for examples of how verbs must match subjects.) Proper nouns—the names of people, companies, cities, etc.—must be capitalized. Sentences must end with terminal punctuation, which usually means a period. Avoid using semicolons, as they tend to confuse people. Use commas to separate items in a list and to provide a breathing break between two long clauses in a sentence. Again, consult the sample resumes for ideas on how to handle specific problems.

# Abbreviations

Abbreviations serve a definite purpose in resumes by allowing more information to be packed into a small space. Use them whenever they can accomplish that purpose without confusing the reader. Always abbreviate the names of states in addresses. (The list of two-letter state abbreviations used by the U.S. Post Office appears below.) You probably should not abbreviate state names elsewhere in your resume. For example, in the sentence "Sales territory included all of northern California," it is better to write out "California" than abbreviate it. And the sentence "Attended University of Idaho for three years" is better than this one: "Attended University of ID for three years." It is permissible, however, to shorten the names of schools if that is how they are commonly known: UCLA, USC, MIT.

One exception to the rule in the preceeding paragraph is when you are including several states in a list. In this example

Have served as assistant to the governor in CA, SD, MI, WA, PA, FL, and MO it is better to abbreviate the states and conserve the considerable space their full names would occupy. Besides, a reader is not likely to be confused when encountering such a list.

Other words may be abbreviated if no confusion is likely to result. A few acceptable ones are: U.S., B.S. (degree), Co. for Company (in a name), Corp. for Corporation (in a name), Inc. for Incorporated (in a name), Nov. for November, mm. for millimeter, lbs. for pounds, and Ave. for Avenue (in an address). In addition, you may use numerous abbreviations and acronyms if you're sure they'll be understood within the context of your resume. FBI is okay if your field is law enforcement. NBC will be understood in the resume of a broadcast journalist. NFL will pass muster if you're a pro linebacker. NEA automatically means National Education Association in a teacher's resume. U.S.F.S. stands for United States Forest Service and is perfectly acceptable in a forest worker's resume. Every trade, occupation, and profession has its own set of acronyms and abbreviations. The rule is this: You may use a short version if there is no chance whatsoever that it will confuse the person who will be reading your resume. If the slightest possibility of confusion exists, write the word(s) out.

### State Abbreviations

| | | | | | |
|---|---|---|---|---|---|
| AK | Alaska | MA | Massachusetts | OR | Oregon |
| AL | Alabama | MD | Maryland | PA | Pennsylvania |
| AR | Arkansas | ME | Maine | PR | Puerto Rico |
| AZ | Arizona | MI | Michigan | RI | Rhode Island |
| CA | California | MN | Minnesota | SC | South Carolina |
| CO | Colorado | MO | Missouri | SD | South Dakota |
| CT | Connecticut | MS | Mississippi | TN | Tennessee |
| DE | Delaware | MT | Montana | TX | Texas |
| FL | Florida | NC | North Carolina | UT | Utah |
| GA | Georgia | ND | North Dakota | VA | Virginia |
| HI | Hawaii | NE | Nebraska | VT | Vermont |
| IA | Iowa | NH | New Hampshire | WA | Washington |
| ID | Idaho | NJ | New Jersey | WI | Wisconsin |
| IL | Illinois | NM | New Mexico | WV | West Virginia |
| IN | Indiana | NV | Nevada | WY | Wyoming |
| KS | Kansas | NY | New York | DC | Dist. of Columbia |
| KY | Kentucky | OH | Ohio | VI | Virgin Islands |
| LA | Louisiana | OK | Oklahoma | | |

# The Editorial Red Pencil

Many professional writers find it much more difficult to write a short article, story, or essay than a long one. Most people can eventually get their message across to a reader if they're allowed to use an unlimited number of words. You're probably no exception. The difficult part about writing, especially resume writing, lies in saying exactly what you need to say in as few words as possible. One way to achieve this economy of words is to do what professionals (in magazines, newspapers, and all other kinds of writing) do: EDIT WHAT YOU WRITE.

Editing is not at all a mysterious, arcane skill. It is simply a matter of going over what has been written and removing what is not essential. Think of the process as excising the fat from a pork chop: you may cut away 30 percent of the chop, but nothing of value is lost. And once the editing is done, what remains carries a greater impact because its message is not buried in rubbish.

Consider this sentence: "I have decided that if I cannot be free, I would rather be dead." Fortunately for us, Patrick Henry was a good editor, and his sentence came out: "Give me liberty or give me death."

If Clark Gable had not had a concise writer behind him when he played Rhett Butler in *Gone With The Wind*, his memorable line might have come out "If you want to know the truth, my dear, I just don't care anymore," instead of "Frankly, my dear, I don't give a damn."

And if Harry Truman had not edited himself, he might have had a sign on his desk that said "People tend to pass the blame for problems on to the next fellow, but when the problem gets to my office, there's nowhere else to pass it." Instead, he said "The buck stops here."

The human tendency to sometimes use too many words affects resume writing too. The "Employment Objective" line on a resume for an x-ray technician could read:

Am looking for position as x-ray technician in a hospital or clinic.

This sounds harmless enough, but it has several unnecessary words in it. Since the name of the section is Employment Objective, it is superfluous to say "Am looking for." A trimmer version would be:

Position as x-ray technician in a hospital or clinic.

This is an improvement, but there's still fat here. Do x-ray technicians work in places other than hospitals or clinics? I suppose some rare ones do, but this reference is probably unneeded. That leaves us with:

Position as x-ray technician.

Now we have a succinct, simple, effective description of the kind of job this person is looking for. That's editing.

Let's look at another example. Consider this job description entry from the resume of a shoe salesperson (the lines are numbered to make discussion of the editing easier):

1  Fitted men, women, and children with
2  shoes, boots, and athletic footwear.
3  Stocked the shelves with shoes when
4  the supply was low. Arranged shoe
5  displays in the front of the store.
6  Conducted inventory of shoes in
7  stock. Assisted the store manager
8  in his job of designing the
9  advertisements for our local
10  newspaper. I even appeared in two
11  TV commercials on station KDUM.

This entry is not very far removed from the kind of writing many people use in their resumes. Let's look at it line by line: (1) "Men, women, and children" could probably be changed to the single word "customers." The fact that this salesperson worked with children may be important because an employer with a large child clientele may need an employee with that skill, so the phrase "of all ages" could be inserted. (2) The single word "shoes" (or "footwear") should be sufficient. (3) Short words such as "the" can often be omitted. Obviously, "shoes" are what was stocked, so that word can be eliminated. (4) Stocking is usually done "when the supply (is) low," so cut that phrase. Again, the word "shoe" is not needed. (5) Displays usually are "in the front of the store," so delete that phrase. (6) The word "took" could be substituted for "conducted" to save a wee bit of space, but "conducted" sounds a little better. There's no need to say "of shoes in stock." What else would be counted in a shoe store? (7) The words "the store" aren't needed. (8) The phrase "his job of" can be cut, as can the article "the." (9) "Our local" can go. (10) Here the resume writer became so excited about his TV appearances that he threw in an "I" that doesn't belong. "Even" can go too. (11) Delete "station KDUM." No one cares which station aired the commercials.

Now, let's see what meat is left after all the fat has been pared away. What remains is a pretty standard kind of entry for a job that is not particularly complex:

> Fitted customers of all ages with shoes. Stocked shelves. Arranged displays. Conducted inventory. Assisted manager in designing advertisements for newspaper. Appeared in two TV commercials.

The words are few, but the message is clear. This entry is packed with powerful, descriptive verbs: fitted, stocked, arranged, conducted, assisted, and appeared. This job might have been routine and uneventful, but the resume entry is strong and solid. Merciless editing made it that way. You should edit the first draft of your resume with the same sharp pencil.

# From "Pride and Joy" to Bureaucratese

Two final suggestions about the language in your resume. First, try to avoid the old, worn-out, overused phrases that seem to work so well for us in our daily speech. They tend to fall flat when committed to paper. A few of these are: pride and joy, acid test, untiring efforts, hale and hearty, on the ball, goes without saying, busy as a bee, supreme sacrifice, slow but sure, few and far between, by leaps and bounds, burning the midnight oil, and after all is said and done. There are dozens more. Don't use them.

Second, beware of gobbledygook, also known as bureaucratese. This is the kind of writing that creeps into resumes in this form: "Supervised the overall procedures for interface between production goals and implementation of sales techniques." Or: "Conducted planning activities aimed at increasing the research productivity related to the management and control of market factors." *What*?

Be yourself. Write in English that is simple, strong, fresh, and understandable.

# Chapter 3

# BUILDING YOUR RESUME

We've mentioned some items that should *not* go in your resume: salary required, reasons for leaving previous jobs, photo. Now it's time to look at the things that ARE found in effective resumes. Very few items absolutely MUST be included in every resume, so let's deal with those first.

## Name

Believe it or not, employers actually have received from job seekers resumes that have no names on them. Such a document, of course, is worthless, so be sure the first thing to go on your resume is your name. Use your full name. If you customarily use a middle initial, use it on your resume too. Do not put a nickname (Shorty, Rocky, Happy) on your resume. You may, however, call yourself Jim instead of James, Bill rather than William, Beth instead of Elizabeth, and so on.

A married woman who wants to include her maiden name on her resume can call herself Sally Davidson McQuiston or Sally (Davidson) McQuiston. Women should be sure to include their maiden names if they were previously employed under that name by a firm to which they are now applying. Also, former employers who may be called upon to provide references may know you only by your maiden name.

Use the title Mr., Ms., or Mrs. on your resume only when (1) you believe it's important that an employer know whether you're a man or a woman *and* (2) your first name does not clearly indicate your sex (as with names such as Pat, Lynn, Chris, Jan, Marian, Fran, and a few others). Legally, employers may not discriminate against you on the basis of your sex, but sometimes it's a good idea to eliminate all possiblity of confusion about whether you're a male or female.

## Address

Always use an address at which you can regularly receive mail. The entire purpose of putting an address on a resume is to allow an employer to write to you offering an interview. And if that invitation is delayed even a few days, your chance of getting the job may be lost. Don't list your home address, for example, if you're going to be in another city attending classes for the summer. Make yourself as available as possible via the U.S. mail. If that means using a friend's address instead of your own, then do it. A college student, who may have two or three different mailing addresses during a year, may be wise to put a parent's address on a resume, knowing the mail will be promptly forwarded.

There's nothing wrong with using a post office box as an address, so long as you check the box regularly. Always include the proper zip code. Never use the kind of address you would give someone who was going to drive to your home (such as "three miles south of Tinyspot, Georgia" or "northwest of Adam's Apple, North Dakota on Route 9").

If you're going to be changing permanent addresses soon after you send out your resumes, you may want to include both the old and the new:

221 S. Fourth W.
Bottin, KY 12345 (before Aug. 10)


or


7 Hickory Ridge Road
Fielding, KY 12367 (after Aug. 10)


# Telephone Number

The advice above goes for telephone numbers too. Don't give a prospective employer your home phone number if no one is likely to be there during the day. After a few tries without an answer, that employer may offer the interview to someone he can reach by phone. It's okay to list a friend's phone number, but tell the friend what you're doing and instruct him/her how you'd like calls handled (which usually means having them take a number for you to call back).

Don't put the phone number of your present place of employment on your resume without first asking your employer if you may. Many companies would get rather upset if they knew you were job hunting on their time. Generally, take calls from prospective employers on your present job only if there is no other way.

You may, if you wish, list a daytime phone number (of a homebound friend, for example) and your own home phone for evening calls. Here's one way to do it:

Phone: 202-345-6677 (daytime message phone)
202-345-2455 (home phone)

Always include your telephone area code, even if you're applying only in your own area. Many firms have headquarters and branches in other places, and it may be someone there who picks up the phone to call you.

Okay, that's it. Name, address, and phone number are the only items that absolutely, positively must go on everyone's resume. Unfortunately, a resume with only that information is never going to get you an interview. What you must do now is give your resume some character by telling of your goals, background, skills, accomplishments, and other things that make you you. No single resume is likely to contain all the different kinds of entries that follow, and you must decide whether your resume will benefit from the inclusion of any particular section.

# Suggested Entries for Chronological Resumes

The suggestions that follow are for resumes that are formatted chronologically. Most people probably should use the standard chronological resume in which dates are prominently displayed and entries work backward through time from the present. Alternatives to the chronological resume are presented in the next chapter, where formatting and page layout are discussed in depth. The following elements are not necessarily listed in the order in which they should appear on your resume. Consult chapter 4 to determine which order might work best for you.

# Employment History

Also called Work History, Employment Background, Experience, or something similar. If you've ever had a job, even a summer or part-time job in high school, you'll want to include this section. By looking at this section, an employer can see what kind of a worker you've been; how many jobs you've had, how long you stayed at each one, what you did on each job, and how that job might relate to the one for which you're applying. For most people, this section is the most important one in the resume.

Begin with your current job. Name your employer and the city in which the business or institution is located. It usually is not necessary to include street addresses. In fact, you probably should avoid listing those addresses so that any potential new employer isn't likely to query your former bosses about you. Later you will provide a list of references, but you should be the one to decide who will be contacted. If the firm's name does not indicate what type of business it is, add a short explanatory blurb such as "paper manufacturer."

Give yourself a job title (being honest, of course), even though you may not actually have been called by that name while on the job. (Succinct, accurate labels help speed the reading of a resume.) List the date you began employment and indicate that you're still working there. The month and year usually are sufficient, and if you've been on the job several years, the month you began becomes irrelevant.

Now, use the forceful, streamlined language we discussed in the previous section to tell what you did on that job. Remember to write primarily with the active verbs that best depict your duties, responsibilities, and accomplishments. Mention any major awards you may have won and honors received. If you were instrumental in effecting changes that benefitted your employer, say so. If you supervised other workers, tell how many. Mention merit promotions. List specialized equipment you learned to operate. If you occasionally functioned as a manager or foreman in that person's absence, say so.

If you were assigned typically managerial duties—payroll computation, banking, advertising, planning, ordering—in a job that was basically not managerial, mention that fact. Be sure to mention your accomplishments on that job: sales increases, money saved, problems solved, training given to new employees, improvements created, new accounts added, and the like. If you can use figures (percents, dollars, etc.) to quantify the feathers in your cap, do so. Make yourself sound as good as possible without stretching the truth.

Mention only the highest level of duties you performed on any job. For example, if you were the night manager in a convenience store and sometimes swept the floor and cleaned the bathrooms, don't bother to list those two tasks. If, as a crackerjack used car salesperson, you had to wash cars and check the air in the tires on slow days, you should not mention those chores in your resume.

All this information should be condensed into one "paragraph" of perhaps 20–70 words. But don't necessarily rely on word count to determine length. Don't worry if the 25-word entry you've just written looks a bit emaciated, as long as you've said everything that needs to be said. It's much more difficult to write a concise description than it is a long one. If you're taking many more than 70 words to describe an uncomplicated job, you probably need to trim off some fat. Keep your language simple and clear. Be as specific as you can, but remember that the person who reads your resume may not be intimately familiar with the daily routine and equipment involved in your job.

Now, repeat the process with the job you held before this one. Here you'll have two dates, the one on which you began work and the one on which you left the job. The verbs you use will now be in past tense. Proceed this way backward through your employment history.

Generally, the farther back you go in time, the fewer words you should be using to describe your job. The farther back you go, the less important that experience becomes. However, if you held a job several years ago that directly relates to the one for which you're applying now, stress that bit of experience and devote proportionately more space to it. For example, if you taught school several years ago, are now driving a cab, and want to get back into teaching, you will want to devote much more resume space to your teaching experience than to your current employment.

If there is one particular aspect of your current job that relates closely to the type of work you're seeking, you should highlight that aspect. Let's say, for instance, that a baker's assistant wants a new job as a retail store clerk. His primary duties have been to bake bread, but he also has assisted customers, run the cash register, calculated per item prices, and arranged displays. He should stress these latter duties and only briefly mention his specific baking chores.

If you acquired some particular knowledge on a job, mention it. But don't feel obligated to say that you came away from each former job with some great new wisdom. Usually, a phrase such as "Became familiar with small-store retail practices," or "Learned to operate heavy equipment" will suffice.

It is not always necessary to include every single job you've ever had. In fact, it probably is a good idea to list only about a half dozen of the jobs you've held. If your employment list goes on and on, it may make you look like an unstable job hopper. If you can backtrack to the time you left high school and list six or fewer jobs, mention them all. If your tally is much higher than that, you may want to group the more ancient jobs into one item, such as this:

    1965–72: Held various farm and ranch jobs.

If at all possible, however, do not present time gaps in your employment history. Try to ACCOUNT FOR ALL TIME SINCE HIGH SCHOOL. A resume that has large time blocks unaccounted for invites prospective employers to wonder if you were in prison, on the lam, or performing burglaries for a living. If your work record indicates that you've had large gaps when you were not gainfully employed, don't try to explain them in your resume. You can do that much more effectively in a cover letter or during an interview (and you may want to consider using a functional resume, explained in Chapter 4).

If you've been out of school for more than just a few years, don't bother to list the summer jobs you held while in high school unless they pertain directly to the position for which you're applying. Truth is, no one in the employment world cares very much about your high school years after you've been out in the real world for a while. If you're a recent high school or college graduate, however, you probably will want to list your summer jobs, because they'll likely be the only work experience you've had. After a few years of full-time employment, you can then drop them from your resume.

If you're a new college or high school graduate and have never held even a regular part-time job, mention the leaf raking, babysitting, lawn mowing, and other things you did to earn money.

Here's how an employment history section might look:

## EMPLOYMENT HISTORY

| | |
|---|---|
| 9/79–Present | Office Manager. Greathouse Realty, Inc., Pittsburgh, PA. Direct activities and schedule shifts for five clerical workers. Coordinate appointments and listings for 14 real estate sales persons. Prepare entries for Multiple Listing publication. Conduct all standard office practices, including correspondence, typing, filing, telephoning, and customer reception. |
| 4/76–8/79 | Secretary. Turner and Associates Insurance Co., Pittsburgh, PA. Served as sole personal secretary to three partners in firm. Wrote letters, handled some claims, greeted customers, and conducted all standard office procedures. Operated micro-computer. Became thoroughly familiar with office practices and insurance business. |
| 2/75–3/76 | Clerk/Typist. Department of Motor Vehicles, Sussex County, VA. Sold auto licenses to public, handled cash, maintained files, and did some light bookkeeping. Occasionally served as temporary shift supervisor. |

# Education

This section may or may not be important in your resume, depending upon your age and the amount of formal education you've had. The purpose here is to give employers a quick summary of your educational accomplishments. Generally, there are two kinds of entries in this section: those pertaining to your high school education and those describing your college or vocational training after high school.

You should include a detailed description of your high school achievements ONLY if you are a recent high school graduate. The longer you've been out of high school, the less you should say about it. If you later graduate from college, you may want to delete information about your high school career altogether. If you do not have a college degree, but it has been 15 years or so since you left high school, your entry here may be pared to the bare bones without robbing your resume of its effectiveness. As you gain employment experience, that experience becomes much more important than anything you did in high school. But until you've been on a full-time job for a few years, your high school accomplishments should be touted. Here's an entry from the resume of a recent high school graduate who did not attend college or vocational school:

## EDUCATION

1977–81:     Fillmore High School, Bainbridge, NH. Maintained B average. Frequently on honor roll. Took electives in algebra, physics, and Spanish. Participated in varsity football for three years and basketball for two. Elected homecoming king as senior. Member student council. Graduated 1981.

A dozen years later, however, that same entry can easily be trimmed to look like this:

## EDUCATION

1977–81:     Fillmore High School, Bainbridge, NH. Graduated 1981.

If you have a college degree, you may want to refrain from referring to your high school days at all. (It's assumed that you went to high school if you've been to college.) Recent college graduates, however, will probably want to keep some reference to their high school careers, because they don't yet have a lengthy work history to fill their resumes.

Unlike a high school entry, the description of your college or vocational school career may change very little through the years. Unlike high school, college and vocational training prepare us for specific types of employment, and employers need to know what post-secondary education we've had. If you have such training, this section will be one of the most important on your resume.

For a college or university, you may include in this section your major and minor fields of study; areas of emphasis within your major; the number of credit hours in a particular study area; the kind of degree earned (B.S., B.A., M.A., etc.); the year you graduated; scholarships you received; your grade point average (if significantly high); honors and awards; quarters or semesters on the dean's list; varsity athletic participation; memberships in fraternities, sororities, and other campus groups; offices held in those groups; other extra-curricular activities; special research projects; and anything else you deem significant about your college career. If you paid for your education yourself by working summers and/or part-time during the school year, mention that fact (it says good things about your character). Separate accomplishments as a graduate student from the description of your undergraduate days.

It is permissible, if you don't have a lot of other information to go in your resume, to list college courses that directly relate to the job for which you're applying. If you're applying outside your major field of study, mention non-major courses that may help qualify you for the job. This course listing should, however, be the first thing to go if your resume starts to get too long.

If you attended more than one college in pursuit of your degree, you may want to name them all. Most emphasis, however, ususally is given to the one from which you graduated. If you attended college but did not graduate, include all the items listed above that apply to you. Indicate how long you attended college. If you graduated from a particularly prestigious institution, you may want to mention that fact in the resume capsule portion of your document.

Be sure to devote some space in your education section to internships, student teaching, practicums, and the like. Experiences here often are more important than many of the other things you did in college.

Most of these principles also apply if you attended a vocational or technical school. Mention equipment you learned to operate, any on-the-job training you received, and the name of the degree or certificate you received.

As with employment history, begin with the current or most recent schools attended and proceed backward through time. Isolated, short courses you've taken after leaving school (perhaps given as training by an employer) may be listed in this section or included with the description of the job to which they apply.

Here's an example of an education section for a new college graduate (including the optional high school entry):

## EDUCATION

| | |
|---|---|
| 1978–82: | University of Kranzburg, Kranzburg, SD. Business major. Psychology minor. 3.8 GPA. Studies emphasized operation of retail business. Received scholarship of $1,000 from U.S. Chamber of Commerce. Ran on varsity track team three years. Member Alpha Sigma Tau Fraternity. Paid for own education by working summers. Wrote senior thesis on planning advertising programs for new businesses. Took some computer programming. Earned B.A. Degree in 1982. |
| 1974–78: | South State Senior High School, Taylor, TN. Took college prep classes. |

# Employment Objective

This section, completely optional, is a very brief statement of what you're looking for in a job. It tells an employer at a glance if your goal and his/her opening are at all compatible. If you use an objective, it should appear near the top of the first page of your resume. As with everything else in your resume, BRIEF IS BEST. This employment objective is too long and vague:

> Seek position in retail store management that will be challenging and will offer opportunity for advancement.

So is this one:

> Am looking for progressive firm in which recently acquired accounting degree may be put to good use.

Virtually everyone wants a job that's challenging, offers the opportunity for advancement, is with a progressive firm, and will put one's training to good use. These two objectives are much better put this way:

> Position in retail store management.

> and

> Position in accounting.

These few words say all that needs to be said. You may, however, have additional SPECIFIC information you want in your objective, such as a geographic area in which you're interested or a specific type of firm you want to work for (see the sample resumes for examples).

People who are qualified to hold vastly different kinds of jobs sometimes have two or more different resumes ready to send out. The only difference may be the stated objective and the order in which education and experience are presented (more about this in the chapter on formatting your resume).

There are advantages and disadvantages to including an "Employment Objective" section. By telling an employer specifically what kind of work you're looking for, your resume will get serious consideration when your goal and his/her opening mesh. The disadvantage is that you may be limiting the kinds of openings for which you'll be considered. If you're willing to take any one of a variety of jobs, you may be better off excluding an objective from your resume.

# Resume Capsule

This summary within a summary, always occuring near the beginning of the resume, tells a reader in just a few words what the entire resume has to say. It's a sort of preview that is used mostly by people who have a rather complex, detailed background. It's also possible to use a capsule if the resume itself outlines qualifications for two different types of occupations. The capsule can warn an employer that such a dichotomy is coming. Unless you have a specific need for a resume capsule, don't use one. If you do include it, you also may call it a "resume summary." Here are two examples:

> Skilled in repair of high voltage power lines and in all aspects of teaching complex electrical principles in classroom.

and

> Have extensive experience in radio and TV production, creation of retail advertising campaigns, and in advertising sales.

# Military

If you've never been on full-time active duty in the Army, Marines, Navy, Air Force, or Coast Guard, don't worry about this section. It isn't necessary to mention participation in the National Guard or other part-time reservist groups unless you are still involved with them.

If you have been in the service, mention the branch, the dates you entered and left, and the kind of discharge you received. If you were an officer, state the highest rank achieved. If enlisted, it probably is better to refrain from mentioning rank, as the designations vary greatly among the service branches and can be quite confusing to civilians. If there is a reason for stating your duty stations (perhaps you're now applying for a job in an area where you lived while in the service), do so but don't list more than three or four. It is not necessary to mention duty stations at all.

Briefly tell what your work was in the military. But avoid the military jargon and verbal shorthand you used in the service. For example, you may have been called a COMSAT REPTECH while on the job. In English that may stand for

Communication Satellite Repair Technician. On your resume you should say you repaired communication satellite equipment. If the work you did in the military is related to the job for which you're now applying, go into as much detail as you would if it had been civilian employment. However, spare the reader of your resume a lengthy description of the electrical work you did on Minuteman missiles if you're now applying for a job as an English teacher.

Mention any significant awards you earned in the service. Presidential Unit Citations probably aren't significant, but Commendation Medals probably are, and Purple Hearts definitely are. Much of the American business world values the military veteran, so don't hesitate to let employers know that you served your country. Here's a sample entry for a Vietnam Air Force Veteran:

## MILITARY

1970–1974:     U.S. Air Force. Served as helicopter mechanic. Spent one year in Vietnam repairing helicopters at remote locations throughout the country. Received two Purple Hearts and Air Force Commendation Medal. Spent last three years at Minot Air Force Base, ND. Honorable discharge.

If you have made a career of the military, you will probably be better off if you treat your years in the service just as you would any other job. That is, list this information under "Experience" or "Employment History" rather than "Military."

# Affiliations and Memberships

Many people have no need for this section on their resumes, but if you belong to numerous noteworthy organizations, here's your chance to say so. There are no dates involved in this section. Simply list the groups of which you're a member and include additional notes (years spent as president, for example) you think may be of interest to a prospective employer.

Now, which organizations should be listed and which should not? That is not an easy question to answer, and you will have to decide for yourself. Here, however, are some suggestions. Don't list groups that require nothing more from you than annual dues or a subscription fee. For example, you should not list the National Geographic Society or Audubon Society or the National Wildlife Federation just because you receive their magazines each month. Sure, you're a member, but it doesn't mean anything to an employer. On the other hand, groups like Lions Clubs, whose members are active in helping underprivileged people, may be mentioned. So may Kiwanis, Rotary, and the other familiar service organizations.

Be sure to mention professional organizations of which you're a member—that is, organizations made up solely of people in your profession. Many teachers belong to the National Education Association. Outdoor writers have the Outdoor Writers Association of America. Doctors have the American Medical Association. And so on. Unions can be included here too. In fact, a prospective employer may be very interested in knowing whether you're a member of a particular union.

If you're applying for work in the same community in which you now live, it may be important to mention the smaller, but locally significant, groups to which you belong, especially the charitable ones. If you are involved in helping single-parent children, the blind, the mentally handicapped, the homeless, the impoverished, the underprivileged, or other needy people, you may wish to say so on your resume. It speaks well of your character to give your time and money to help other people, and the employer who reads your resume may even be a member or benefactor of the same groups. You also may mention parent-teacher organizations, Boy and Girl Scouts, alumni associations, and other notable volunteer groups that perform some sort of public service. If the group is not well known, you may need to add a brief explanation of what it does. Church affiliations usually are not mentioned, although significant church work within the community may be touted without mentioning the church denomination.

Two warnings are in order here. FIRST, don't include this section in your resume unless you have several groups to mention. A list that proclaims your memberships and affiliations and has only two entries is like damning with faint praise. If you can't mention at least four affiliations, don't list any at all (except for professional organizations, which should always be listed, regardless of number). SECOND, don't list too many groups. The longer your list of memberships becomes, the more it clutters your resume. And an employer may begin to wonder if you'll even have time to do your job. Listing five or six is about right. Here's what this section may look like:

MEMBERSHIPS AND AFFILIATIONS

Teamsters Union

Boy Scout leader

Westside Lions Club (President)

Big Brothers and Sisters

Print Handicapped Radio Reading Service

# Publications

Few people include this section in their resumes, simply because few people have ever had any of their writing published. If you have had something published (outside of a high school or college publication) you may want to mention it. This can be important if writing will be part of the job for which you're applying. Books, magazines, scholarly journals, and newspapers are the most common media in which people get published, but if you've written movie scripts, pamphlets or other things, they can be mentioned too. You also could include in this section any photographs and drawings of yours that have appeared in a book, magazine, or other publication. Do not list unpublished writings, such as that novel you may have tucked away in your desk drawer.

You probably will want to include a publications section only if (1) you have been published in prestigious places, (2) writing will be an important part of the job for which you're applying, or (3) you have had many articles, books, etc. published. Just as with memberships and affiliations, one or two isolated entries probably won't do much to enhance your resume and should be left out.

If, however, you have been published many times, you may not be able to list all the entries on your resume. The best thing to do then is to mention a few of the more prestigious publications and then simply say that a more detailed portfolio is available upon request.

Here's what this section might look like on the resume of a person who has been freelancing magazine articles part time:

PUBLICATIONS

> *National Wildlife*—article—April–May, 1983
> *Audubon*—photos—November, 1982
> *Family Circle*—article—January, 1982
> *Science Digest*—article and photos—December, 1981
> Many other publications. Portfolio available on request.

# Personal Information

One optional section that most people like to put in their resumes is a brief sketch of their personal lives. The purpose of this section is to give the reader of your resume a glimpse of you as a person, not just as a potential worker. Items here may include your date of birth, marital status, health, willingness to travel on a job, willingness to relocate, languages spoken, height, weight, hobbies, and whether you own your home. The personal section of your resume, if you decide to include one, need not contain all these items. Let's take a look at them one at a time.

DATE OF BIRTH. This allows you to tell an employer how old you are. It may be illegal for an employer to ask your age, but there's nothing to stop you from volunteering that information if you think it will be to your advantage to do so. If, however, you think your chances for an interview will diminish if the employer knows how old you are, leave this item out. For example, a person over 50 who is applying for an entry-level position (such as a housewife entering the job market for the first time) may be better off not mentioning her age. This item will NOT be conspicuous by its absence if it is not included. Always express your age as date of birth, not as 24 or 38 or 44 or whatever. This way, your resume will not have to be retyped after your next birthday.

MARITAL STATUS. Some people believe that the "proper" information here enhances employment possibilities, but the advantage can go either way. Let's say that a firm is looking for a solid citizen who's likely to remain with the company for a long time in one location. There may be a tendency on the part of the employer to think (fairly or unfairly) that a married worker with two children more completely fills that bill than a single person who may have fewer ties to a job and a community. If, however, the firm is in need of someone to spend five nights a week on the road and some weekends in the office, a single person without the demands of a family to conflict with the job may have the edge. You decide for yourself. If you do include this item, simply say that you are married or single. The word "divorced" still conjures up negative images in some minds and is best avoided. The fact that you are a widow or widower is not important and should not be mentioned. If you wish to let the employer know that you have children, do it this way: Marital Status: married; two children.

HEALTH. A single word, either "excellent" or "good," is all you should ever say here. You are not obligated to comment on your health, and to do so when your condition is only fair or poor is to hurt your job chances. If you can't, in good faith, say that you're in excellent or good health, don't say anything. And a resume is no place to attempt to explain complex health conditions that may or may not affect your job performance. If you do have a definite health problem or handicap such as deafness, a heart condition, loss of some eyesight, or loss of limbs, explain that problem (and its potential effect on your ability to do a job) in a cover letter to your resume or save it for the interview.

WILLINGNESS TO TRAVEL. Not everyone is willing to hit the road for a few days each week. If you are, and if you know or suspect that travel may be part of the job for which you're applying, say so. You can simply say that you're willing to travel, or you can suggest some limits, such as three days per week. Or, you can be intentionally vague and say you'll do "some" traveling on the job. Indicating that you're available for travel may give you a slight edge over competitors who make no reference to the subject. Again, if you can't say something here that will boost your interview chances, say nothing at all.

WILLINGNESS TO RELOCATE. This is a tougher question than that of travel. Are you really willing to sell your house, leave your friends, take your children out of school, and move to Antelope Bend, Grits Hollow, Scarsdale, or wherever? Many employers desire this mobility in the people they hire. Even if the current opening is in your own community, many firms have other branches and make a practice of periodically shuffling employees from one plant to another. If you're honestly willing to pack up and move if you get the job, say so on your resume. And you may qualify your willingness to relocate by specifying a particular geographic area. For example, "Willing to relocate anywhere in the South."

LANGUAGES SPOKEN. Are you FLUENT in any language besides English? If so, mention this fact even though you may not see how it will enhance your job possibilities. Very few Americans are fluent in two or more languages, which makes bilingual applicants rare. Who knows, that company with an office around the corner from your house may also have an office in Japan, extensive dealings with German manufacturers, many Mexican workers in Arizona, and research affiliations in France. Being able to speak Japanese, German, Spanish, or French may be just enough to tip the scales in your favor. Do not, however, claim to be bilingual if your training in a second language is limited to a couple of high school or college classes. Unless you can converse with a native speaker or read the language with complete comprehension, skip this entry.

HEIGHT AND WEIGHT. This is a totally optional item that probably should be included only if there is a specific reason to do so. If you're applying for a job as a stevedore, you may want to let the employer know that you're 6 feet, 4 inches tall and weight 240 pounds. Conversely, a ballerina may wish to advertise that she's a petite 5 feet and 95 pounds. The questions to ask yourself are these: Will height and weight likely be a factor the employer considers when filling the position? Will it be to my advantage to tell the employer my height and weight? If the answer to both questions is "yes," go ahead and include these two vital statistics in your resume.

INTERESTS. This is another purely optional item. It could also be labeled HOBBIES. Its purpose is to show that you are a well-rounded individual with diverse interests. This section will not be missed if you leave it out, and it isn't likely to contribute a great deal if included. If you have room, feel free to tell an employer that you enjoy tennis, reading mystery novels, gourmet cooking, stamp collecting, hunting, sewing, or whatever occupies your spare time. If you include this section, mention at least three and no more than six leisure-time activities. Volunteer work could be mentioned here if you have not already included it under Affiliations and Memberships. Try to show some variety in your interests.

HOME OWNERSHIP. Another very optional item. The fact that you (along with the bank) own your home indicates some tie to the community and some degree of stability in your life. If you think these are attributes an employer is looking for, mention your home ownership.

ITEMS YOU SHOULD *NOT* INCLUDE IN THIS SECTION: (1) Occupation, position, titles, or any other information about your spouse, father, mother, siblings, or anyone else; (2) Your financial condition; (3) Equipment you own;

(4) Physical characteristics such as the condition of your teeth, your voice quality, color of your hair, or body measurements (other than height and weight); (5) The fact that you are engaged to be married; or (6) The number of cars you own.

Don't laugh, some resume books suggest you include such information. And, of course, there's an endless list of other items that have no place in your resume. Occasionally, however, the requirements of a certain job may lead you to include a bit of personal information you would normally leave out. (Perhaps you're applying for a position as zookeeper and wish to mention that you have no known allergies and that you like animals.) Always ask yourself WHY you're including a particular item.

All put together, here's what a personal information section may look like:

## PERSONAL

Born: March 7, 1946                       Marital Status: Single

Health: Excellent                          Height: 6'; Weight: 175 lbs.

Own home

Willing to Relocate and to travel

Interests: Hunting, chess, church work, photography

# Certifications

This section will apply only to those people who must meet some specific requirements before being allowed to practice their profession or fully provide a service. Accountants take a test to become certified, nurses must be registered, pilots must be licensed, lawyers must pass a bar examination, teachers earn certificates, and so on. If yours is a profession that does not require such certification, you will not include this section. If, however, you do possess the certificate or license or registration that is part of your profession, it should be mentioned in your resume. State the specific certification you have earned. If you've recently passed a one-time or periodic test to obtain that certification, you may wish to mention the date of the test. Don't include in this section common certifications such as a regular driver's license. Here are a couple of examples, first for a teacher and then for an accountant:

## CERTIFICATION
Hold secondary teaching certificates for Maine and New Hampshire. Endorsed in English and math. Both certificates expire June 1986.

and

## CERTIFICATION
Passed all portions of C.P.A. examination in May, 1983.

# General

This is an optional, catchall category into which you may put any pertinent information that just didn't seem to fit anywhere else. If you decide to include this section, make sure its contents have some relationship to the job for which you're applying. Don't include information just to fill up space. Some possibilities for the general section include your background (Did you grow up in the inner city or in a town of 500?), how you get along with people, your personality characteristics, equipment and tools you can bring with you to the job, special skills you've developed, and your attitude toward work. There are, of course, many more items that could be included, depending upon the type of job you're seeking. One such section—from the resume of a person applying for a job selling livestock feed to farmers—might look like this:

### GENERAL
Grew up on farm and am thoroughly familiar with modern methods of raising livestock. Have outgoing personality. Am aggressive salesperson who knows how to close a sale. Willing to work long hours. Am quick learner.

Here's another general section, this time from the resume of a waitress:

### GENERAL
Grew up in family that operated large restaurant. Enjoy meeting people. Have excellent memory and good head for figures. Work well under pressure. Take pride in personal appearance.

# References

This section has become the traditional last entry in nearly everyone's resume. In its best, simplest form, the section consists solely of this line: REFERENCES: Available Upon Request.

Good references are an important part of every job seeker's arsenal. But the specific names, addresses, and phone numbers of the references should not go on your resume. It is enough to inform a prospective employer that they exist. After that employer has formed an opinion about you, usually after your interview, he/she may ask you to provide the names of a few (2–4) references.

Good prospects for references are former employers with whom you had a good relationship, present or former teachers, pastors, business associates, and personal friends. Even before you begin disseminating your resume, you should contact these people to ask if they'll be willing to share their thoughts about you with prospective employers. At this time you also can verify their correct phone numbers and addresses. As soon as your resume goes out, you should be ready to provide your list of references to interested employers.

Choose your references carefully, as their opinions of you may weigh heavily in an employer's decision whether to hire you. Don't take former employers for granted. They may not have been as pleased with your performance as you thought, and if it's been a while they may not remember much about you. Call or visit each potential reference before passing his/her name on to a potential new employer. You should, as a matter of courtesy, ask the person if he/she is willing to speak on your behalf.

# Chapter 4

# CHOOSING A RESUME FORMAT

Through the ages, employers have been bombarded with resumes in all imaginable sizes, shapes, colors, and forms. One hotshot job seeker is said to have typed across the top of his resume the line "I'm Too Hot To Pass Up" and then took a cigarette lighter and burned all the edges of the document. History has not recorded whether he got the job with his attention-getting technique. I'm told that one woman obtained a job as a canoe trip guide by inscribing her resume on the blade of a canoe paddle. A would-be disk jockey committed his resume onto a cassette tape. Ploys like these may occasionally succeed, and we'll discuss creative resumes later in this chapter.

Most employers, however, have come to expect job seekers to structure their resumes in more familiar ways. There is more than a little disagreement in the business world about what constitutes a good resume. A resume that gets one employer jumping for joy may totally bore the next person. While there are few hard and fast rules governing the format your resume may take, two guidelines stand out above all others: An employer must find your resume easy to read, and he/she must be able to read it quickly. You should keep these two criteria always in mind when writing and formatting your resume.

For nearly all job seekers, the question of acceptable resume format comes down to two choices: chronological or functional. The information contained in the resume will be essentially the same under both formats, but its arrangement and the emphasis it is given will differ slightly. Let's look at these two separately.

## Chronological Resume

The word chronology means "time," and what you'll be doing in a chronological resume is summarizing your background by time period. This is the kind of resume whose elements we were constructing in the last section. The complete resume that follows is an example of typical chronological resume format:

JANE RUTHERFORD

1000 Blue Star Lane
Crown Heights, MA 09090                    Telephone: (213)656-1111

*Objective*

Position as country club social director.

*Education*

1979–1983:    Simmons University, Richmond, MA. Earned M.A. in sociology. As teaching assistant, taught classes in introductory sociology. 4.0 GPA. Awarded State Scholarship. Wrote thesis on the role of Irish immigrants in the development of the history of Boston.

1975–1979:    Grant College, Prescott, NH. Genetics major. Literature minor. Graduated Suma Cum Laude in 1979 with B.A. Degree. Participated in women's varsity soccer program for three years. Member Beta Kappa Epsilon Sorority.

### *Experience*

1981–1983:    WAITRESS, University Food Service, Richmond, MA. Served food to students in campus dining hall. Regularly served as vegetable supervisor.

1979–1981:    DORM MAID, University Housing, Richmond, MA. Made beds, swept rooms, dusted chairs, and performed other cleaning duties in 200-room dorm.

1977–1979:    SALESPERSON, Billy's Record Shop, Prescott, NH. Helped customers in selecting and choosing their purchases.

### *Personal*

Born: January 1, 1957                                    Health: Excellent
Marital Status: Single
Interests: Stock market, babysitting, auto racing, soccer

### *References*

Excellent references available on request.

This kind of resume works best for nearly all people. This is the format most employers expect to see when they settle down to browse a stack of resumes. If you have been in school or employed in relatively few jobs since you became an adult, this is the kind of resume you probably should use. The open, straightforward presentation of the dates allows a reader to see at a glance how you've spent your life. This also is the easiest type of resume to write. Now, let's look at how this kind of resume becomes married to a sheet of paper.

In your resume, the most important items will be your name, address, and phone number. With these bits of information staring an employer in the face, it's a simple matter for him/her to call or write asking you to stop by for a visit. Therefore, these three items should be displayed prominently at the top of the page. You may wish to type your name all in capital letters to make it stand out. It doesn't matter whether your name, address, and phone number are centered, on the left margin, or arranged some other way. Just be sure they are displayed prominently and the positioning is attractive and uncluttered. You may, if you like, place the word "RESUME" above your name; some people prefer the phrase "Resume of" before their names. Suit yourself.

Next will come your occupational objective and/or resume capsule, if you choose to use those sections. Keep them brief so they don't detain an employer en route to the more important parts of your resume—your background.

## Which Comes First?

The two most important sections in your chronological resume will be those describing your work history and your education. Which, you ask, should come first? That depends upon which is more likely to convince the employer that you should be granted an interview. Which section says things about you that most directly qualify you for this job? Which section speaks to the employer and says "Hire this person"? Put that section first. Which of your qualifications are most closely related to the position for which you're applying? Stress these. A few examples may make this clearer.

If you have not been to college or vocational school, list your employment record first, even though it may cover only part-time or summer jobs. High school academic records don't carry a lot of weight in the employment world, so they shouldn't be used to lead off the important part of a resume unless you have no work record at all to draw upon.

If you have just graduated from college with a degree in biology and are looking for a job as a biologist, list your education first. But, if you are applying for permanent employment at the convenience store where you worked for three years while in college, list your employment experience first.

If you are applying for a position as an accountant, have a degree in accounting, and have five years of accounting experience, list your experience first. (Experience usually means more than academic training.)

If you have graduated from a vocational school's secretarial program, have extensive experience as a waitress, and are applying as a clerk-typist, list your education first.

If you have been out of college with a music degree for more than a few years, have been employed as a salesperson for all that time, and are seeking a job as a salesperson, list your experience first. If, however, you've decided to apply for a position as a music teacher, list your education first.

What it all comes down to is this: List first whichever information is most closely related to the job you're seeking and more likely to impress an employer. And remember that the value of educational accomplishments tends to fade as the years pass. There is no good substitute for firsthand job experience.

## The Dating Game

The two most important sections of your chronological resume—experience and education—are based on the dates you began and ended each job or stint in school. You begin with the present or most recent item and work backward through your school and work history. Usually, the year alone is sufficient, but if you can include the month, do so. But be consistent: either include the month all the time (within a given employment section) or don't use the month at all. Sometimes, such as with summer employment, it is definitely better to include the month you began and ended work. Your beginning and ending dates, then, for a summer job while in college might be 6/82–9/82. It saves space to use numerals rather than the names of the months.

Everyone knows that the school year begins in the fall and ends in the spring, so it is not really necessary to specify the months when listing your years in high school and college. Those dates might simply be 1979–1983. (Or, you may do it this way: 1979–83.)

The most important thing to remember about a chronological resume is that, if possible, all your time since high school should be accounted for. Large gaps in time can function as red flags to prospective employers, who may wonder just what you were doing in those missing years. Short gaps, however, carry virtually no stigma and need not be explained. It's not uncommon for hard-working people to travel, be unemployed, or simply take a hiatus for several months, so don't feel obligated to account for every single month.

And short gaps often can be camouflaged by the judicious use of dates. Let's say that in February, 1975, you quit a good job with ABC Co. after five years of employment. You then spent the next 18 months (until August, 1976) traveling. Then you returned to the workaday world with XYZ Co. and stayed with that firm for five years. Your resume entry for ABC Co. could accurately state that you were employed by that firm from 1970 to 1975. It could also state that you were employed by XYZ Co. from 1976 to 1981. Your long vaction has been excised from your resume. Of course, you should not lie about the period of unemployment if asked directly, but for resume purposes you have eliminated the gap.

If you have a large, unavoidable gap in your work record due to serious illness, time in prison, long-term unemployment, or other causes, don't try to explain it on your resume. Simply allow the gap to occur on your resume and then briefly account for it honestly in your cover letter or wait to discuss it in an interview. Or, you may wish to get away from dates entirely by writing a functional rather than a chronological resume (see below).

Time period by time period, you'll work your way backward through your employment and educational history. If you've listed your employment experience first, then your education section should follow, and vice versa. This is the meat of your resume, so spend the most time on these two sections.

The dates need not appear at the left margin. They also can be listed at the beginning or at the end of an entry. You may even come up with some new way of positioning the dates. Just be sure they allow an employer to move step by step through your background. That, after all, is the purpose of a chronological resume.

## The Rest Of The Story

Next should come the short sections titled MILITARY, GENERAL, CERTIFICATIONS, AFFILIATIONS AND MEMBERSHIPS, PUBLICATIONS, and any others you may choose to include. Usually, the PERSONAL and REFERENCES sections work best when they follow each other in that order at the end of a resume. There are, however, no definite rules for the placement of any of these less important parts of your resume. Whatever order works best for you is the order to use. Make certain, though, that you use parallel construction for the labeling of each section. That is, if you underline or capitalize one section heading, do the same for all of them.

# Functional Resume

This brings us to the one good alternative available to the chronological resume: the functional resume. You may want to consider using the functional version if (1) you have large gaps of unemployment in your work history, (2) you have a history as a job hopper (never staying very long on one job), (3) you have acquired skills and abilities that cannot be tied to any particular jobs you've had, or (4) you have skills in distinctly different areas.

A functional resume differs from the chronological only in the way your employment history is handled. Instead of describing each individual job you've had and telling exactly how long you held it, you will look at those jobs as a whole and tell an employer *What you can do now*. You may mention former employers and dates of employment somewhere on the resume, but this information will clearly be secondary to the general CAN DO theme. This way, valuable experience garnered in many places may be consolidated and presented as one strong skill. Gaps of unemployment become much less prominent. And a history of job hopping need not be detailed. All other sections of your resume—education, personal, military, general, etc.—will probably be handled the same way as in the chronological version.

Here's what a functional resume might look like for a restaurant cook and assistant manager who has worked for 17 different restaurants in the past four years (not exactly an employment record he'd like to publicize):

## JACK MALONE

2222 Tower Road
Saunders, Missouri 99876                     Telephone (123)444-8792

### OBJECTIVE

Position as restaurant assistant manager or as cook.

### QUALIFICATIONS

Managerial:     Have extensive experience as assistant manager of small and medium-size restaurants. Hire and fire, prepare work schedules, order supplies, design menus, bank receipts, and handle complaining customers. Know how to coordinate the work of cooks, waitresses, and busboys. Capable of maintaining high worker morale and universal customer satisfaction. Can manage restaurant indefinitely without supervision.

Cook:          Can prepare all kinds of restaurant food, from gourmet to hamburgers. Familiar with modern restaurant cooking facilities. Know the value of preparing food precisely as ordered and as quickly as possible. Work well with other cooks and under pressure.

### Employers

The Village Inn, Sacramento, CA
Don's Family Restaurant, Sacramento, CA
The Blue Sword Supper Club, San Diego, CA
El Matador, Bridgeport, NJ
Mr. Steak, Newton, NJ

### Education

Monmouth County High School, Newton Hills, PA. Graduated 1977.

### Personal

Born: July 9, 1959                     Health: Excellent
Height: 6'; Weight 170 lbs.            Marital Status: Single
Interests: Bowling, reading, fishing, swimming

### References

Available on request

As you can see, only the employment section is appreciably different from that of a chronological resume. The man's qualifications stand out but his job-hopping past does not. No dates are given. Many functional resumes do, however, carry some dates of employment, often "buried" at the ends of lines or paragraphs. This is what you should do if you want to include dates but don't want to emphasize them. It's also possible to quantify your job history without listing specific dates. At the end of a paragraph, instead of listing dates, you could say "Two years" or "Six years" or whatever the total of that job experience came to. This way, employers get an idea of the depth of your experience, but you don't have to reveal specific dates.

Notice, too, that Jack Malone does not list all his previous employers. Since this kind of resume is not meant to be a year-by-year accounting of one's past, it's not necessary that all former jobs be mentioned.

Here are the pertinent sections from another functional resume, this time for a woman who has never had a full-time job but who has marketable skills just the same:

## OCCUPATIONAL OBJECTIVE

Position as retail clerk or office assistant.

### QUALIFICATIONS

| | |
|---|---|
| Retail: | Grew up in family which operated clothing store. Throughout high school assisted parents with all aspects of store management. Set up displays, assisted customers, ran cash register, and took inventory. Thoroughly familiar with duties of a retail clerk. |
| Office: | For past 11 years handled most clerical chores for husband's small business. Conducted correspondence, kept books, computed taxes, filed, and took telephone messages. Accomplished all this in the home while raising two children. Type 70 words per minute and operate 10-key adder. |

If full-time, paid jobs were all this lady could put on her resume, it would be a bleak document indeed. The functional approach has given her a chance to tout her skills. Other examples of functional resumes appear in Chapter 6 of this book.

# Creative Resume

Unless you have an overriding, urgent need to be creative with your resume, DON'T. Most attempts at writing a creative resume fail miserably. What you think is creative may be perceived as smart-alecky and disrespectful by a staid, conservative employer. Most people have nothing in their backgrounds that cannot be adequately and effectively conveyed via the chronological or functional approach.

The only job seekers who should even consider a creative resume are those who (1) are applying for jobs that demand creativity (those in advertising, entertainment, graphics, the arts, etc.) or (2) are applying in other fields to firms that have a reputation for nonconformity and creativity. Most employers are looking for someone to fit into a mold, fill a slot, staff a position. Most firms aren't in the market for free souls who may give them headaches by insisting they be allowed to "do their own thing."

A creative resume is, in essence, any resume that deviates markedly in either form or content from the two types we've already discussed. The canoeist's paddle and the disk jockey's tape are two extreme examples. Regardless of how creative you get, your goal still must be to tell the reader about yourself. If your creativity is all that comes across, then your resume becomes a sample of your work and nothing more.

Now, how can you get creative? If you're trying to sell your skills as an artist, you could TASTEFULLY AND IN A SUBDUED MANNER include a sketch or two on your resume. If you simply want to advertise your individuality, you could have your resume printed in white ink on black paper (more about colored paper later). If you're a musician, you could arc some musical notes across the top of the page. If you're a calligrapher, you could produce the entire document in beautiful curled writing. If you're a journalist, you could proclaim your talents with a headline emblazoned across the page. Ideas for creative resumes are limited only by your own creativity. But remember, a creative resume stands a good chance of turning people off, not on.

On a less drastic level, you could have your resume professionally typeset so that you can employ two or three different type sizes and styles. (For example, you could print part of your document in italics.) You might have the highlights appear in boldface type, or you could use horizontal and vertical lines to separate the parts of your resume. You could arrange the information—the description of a job, for example—in list form instead of paragraph form. If you feel you must go creative, subtle variations like these stand a better chance of keeping your resume on an employer's desk and out of the waste basket. Here's one example of what a slightly creative resume might look like (a few other examples can be found in Chapter 6):

OUTDOOR WRITER     OUTDOOR WRITER     OUTDOOR WRITER

Richard Boulton
1818 Mountain Ridge Place
Denver, Colorado 65790

—— I WANT TO WRITE FOR YOU ——

| | |
|---|---|
| Experience: | ● Articles in *Outdoor Life, Sports Afield*, and *Field and Stream*. |
| | ● Three years as outdoor editor of Salem Daily Herald Newspaper, Salem, OR. |
| | ● Columns appear regularly in eleven daily newspapers across the country. |
| | ● Take photos to accompany articles. |
| Education: | ● M.A. in journalism, University of Idaho, 1980. |
| | ● B.S. in wildlife biology, Arizona State University, 1975. |
| Publications: | ● Excellent portfolio available upon request. |

Personal:
- Born August 3, 1955
- Health Excellent
- Married
- Will relocate

References:
- Available upon request

OUTDOOR WRITER    OUTDOOR WRITER    OUTDOOR WRITER

# Make It Pretty

The cardinal rule to remember when you come to actually putting your resume in its final form is to MAKE IT APPEALING TO THE EYE. First impressions are tremendously important, and your resume will be solely responsible for whatever first impression a prospective employer forms of you. You have to make that employer feel good about you from the very beginning, and the best way to do that is to give him/her a resume that reeks of forethought, organization, neatness, balance, logic, and—yes—beauty.

Don't crowd the type. Leave plenty of white space on all sides and between sections within the resume. Leave a margin of 1 to 1¼ inches on all sides. Remember, this document you're creating is an advertisement that must attract and hold a reader's attention. Your goal is to present a complete and attractive package, not cram as much information as you can onto a sheet of paper.

On a normal typewriter, the bulk of your resume should be single spaced, with double and triple spacing between sections and parts of sections. Remember that, if possible, you should hold your resume to a single page and try not to exceed two pages. If the first draft of your precious document is just slightly more than one page, try editing it a bit so that you don't end up with a second page containing only a line or two. And don't divide a section between two pages; put ALL of your military or educational or publication information on the first page, and then start the second page with a new section. Be sure your name appears at the top of EVERY resume page.

You also may use underlining and capital letters to lend a dash of character to your resume. Use these liberally to break up what could otherwise be monotonous type. You may underline and/or capitalize (that is, write entirely in capital letters) the names of the resume sections, the specific skills you have to offer, your job titles during past employment, former employers, the names of universities you have attended, degrees you've earned, or most anything else you deem important. Just be sure to remain consistent throughout your resume. If you underline the word "Experience," you also should underline "Education," "Personal," and so on. If you type one employer's name all in capital letters, do so for the others too.

When you have written the last draft of your resume and are ready for the final typing, you may wish to have someone else read it. If you know someone in a management position who is familiar with resumes, ask for an honest appraisal of the document in general. If nothing else, have a spouse or friend proofread it for grammar, spelling, and punctuation errors.

When it comes time to do the final typing and reproduction of copies, don't be cheap. You bought this book and put several hours into writing a top-notch resume. Don't negate all the work you've done by trying to save a few cents or minutes on the mechanics of getting your resume completed.

If at all possible, have your resume typed on an electric typewriter, so that all keystrokes are made with equal force. Manual typewriters frequently produce images of varying blackness and density, and this can look shoddy. If you're doing your own typing, break down and buy a new typewriter ribbon for this occasion. Also clean the typewriter keys. If you're hiring a typist, ask to see samples from his/her typewriter. Most cartridge style typewriters can use a carbon film cartridge that produces an image that is noticeably sharper than that made by a standard ribbon. Ask about it.

Depending upon how many copies of your resume you'll need, you may wish to consider sending individually typed resumes to each prospective employer. If you decide to do this, have the resume typed on a self-correcting typewriter (the kind that can lift mistakes off the page, not just cover them up). Don't send out a resume with mistakes corrected with white fluid or correction cover-up tape.

Word processors are becoming quite common, and these little gems can produce perfect, individually typed copies every time. However, be sure that the typing appears to have been done by a standard (pica or elite) typewriter. Don't let anyone talk you into having your resume typed by a dot printer (these printers produce the "computer readout" kind of typing in which each letter is made up of tiny dots). Professional typing or word processing will cost more than doing it yourself, but usually it's worth it if you plan to send out individually typed copies.

Most job seekers, though, send employers GOOD QUALITY photocopies of their resumes. This is probably what you will want to do if you're disseminating more than just a few resumes. This way you can save some money by typing the original yourself, because neatness of corrections is not important (as long as there are no black marks on the page). Copiers only pick up black and white, not the unsightly blotches of dried correction fluid.

Copy shops abound in most cities, and their per copy cost of producing your resume should not be exorbitant. If you need more than 25 copies, ask about having them printed offset, as this will be even cheaper than photocopying. Never send out fuzzy or cheap-looking photocopies.

Regardless of the reproduction process you use, DON'T SKIMP ON PAPER QUALITY. Don't, for example, have your resumes printed on the same standard photocopy paper you'd use if you were making a file copy of your income tax forms. Ask to see a copy shop's selection of papers, and choose one that looks and feels classy and expensive. It will cost you a few cents more per sheet, but it will be worth it. Use only 8½-by-11-inch bond (which means high quality) paper at least 20 pounds in weight (a designation of relative thickness). If you want really high quality, get a paper that has a cotton (rag) content of 25 percent or greater. Papers come in a variety of finishes. Choose one that you think will appeal to the readers of your resume.

Resumes typically are printed with black ink on white paper. It's probably a good idea to keep the black ink, but you may wish to put your resume on colored paper. The reasoning (never proven, however) is this: A busy employer or personnel director, facing a stack of 100 resumes, will reach past 99 white ones to pick up the one on colored paper. Your colored resume, theoretically, may get read before those belonging to your competitors.

But you should be careful about the color of the paper you use. Keep the hue as subdued as possible. Select a soft beige, gray, tan, off-white, very subtle blue, or other muted pastel. Never put your resume on bright, loud paper. Remember, you want to soothe the tired eye of the employer, not shock him/her into submission.

One final mechanical suggestion: Whenever possible, try to get your resume into an employer's hands in a flat, unfolded condition. Hand deliver them if practical. When mailing your resumes, send them flat in 9-by-12-inch envelopes. This resume you've labored so hard to produce is your ticket to an interview and possibly a new job. Treat it with care, and it will do (and get) the job for you.

# Chapter 5

# THE COVER LETTER

No resume should ever be forced to venture alone into the business world. Just as you will not go naked to your job interviews, so must the resumes you mail be properly covered en route to employers' waiting hands. Except for the resumes you may hand carry to employers, every one you send out should be accompanied by a brief missive called a cover letter.

A cover letter is important for several reasons. First, it shows that you are a courteous individual. It has long been standard practice in the employment-seeking ritual to address a letter to the person you are asking to read your resume. You are, after all, trying to sell something to that person, and you will want to begin your relationship on the very best footing. Even if your letter contains no information above and beyond that found in your resume (which is unlikely), you still should write a cover letter just as an act of courtesy. Quite simply, this is the way job hunting through the mail is done, and employers are apt to look askance at unsolicited resumes arriving without their proper covering.

Even more important, however, cover letters allow you to highlight and elaborate upon information contained in your resume. You have an opportunity in your cover letter to "hit 'em again" with your best punch, restating your most impressive qualifications. Resumes should stick mainly to the facts, but in a letter you can make a highly biased sales pitch for yourself. You have an opportunity here to tell a specific employer exactly why you are sending a resume to him/her and exactly why he/she should be interested in learning more about you. Theoretically, your cover letter will garner for you a few minutes of undivided attention from the person in whose hands your future may be held. A well-written cover letter can make an employer eager to take a look at your resume.

Also, you may use your cover letter to convey factual information for which there was not room or an appropriate place in your resume. You may discuss acquaintances you have in common, your availability for an interview, or a physical handicap you have overcome. You can tell an employer about your father's lifelong employment with the firm, your own special interest in the industry, or anything else you deem important. Your cover letter can be a means of conveying the many tidbits you'd like an employer to know about you.

Finally, your cover letter can serve as a sample of your verbal abilities and your knowledge of standard business communications practices. If you will be expected to do any sort of writing on your new job, your employer will naturally be wondering about your written English skills. Unlike your resume, a cover letter is composed of sentences and paragraphs, all capitalized and punctuated according to the rules of standard written English. If your letter follows accepted guidelines for business communications and if your grammar, usage, spelling, and punctuation are error-free, you are likely to make a favorable impression on an employer. Such a letter will immediately set you apart from many of your competitors.

# Conform to the Norm in Form

If you are familiar with standard business letter format, you already know how to structure your cover letter. If you're already using the correct style, your cover letter can be written in the same format as the business letters you use to complain about a product, order merchandise, or solicit information. There is no secret structure for a cover letter, other than that it must conform to standard business letter format. The sample letters at the end of this section employ that format.

Whenever possible, address your cover letter to a particular individual, the one who has the authority to grant you an interview. In a small firm, this will be the manager or even the owner. In a larger business, it may be someone with the title of personnel director. You usually can obtain the proper person's name (and the correct spelling) by calling the company or institution and asking a secretary. You'll likely receive the information you need without even being asked why you want it.

Don't rely on information from a friend, newspaper article, want ad, or other source when you're addressing your letter. Be absolutely certain you're writing to the proper person, and be just as certain that you're spelling his/her name correctly.

If you absolutely cannot learn the name of the proper person, address your letter by job title to an office, such as Personnel Director, Manager, or District Supervisor. NEVER address a business letter to this person: To Whom It May Concern.

The salutation of your cover letter is important too. Thousands of employers have received letters from job seekers who obviously did not know how to spell the employer's names—or even if they were men or women. For example, mistakenly using the salutation "Dear Mrs. Olson" to address a man named Lynn Olsen is not likely to endear you to Mr. Olsen. The sender of such a letter automatically is at a disadvantage in dealing with that person, so be accurate at all costs.

Unless you already have a first-name relationship with the person, use the designations Mr., Mrs., or Ms. in your salutation. Unless you are certain that a woman prefers the "Mrs." form of address, use "Ms." Many married women prefer the "Ms." form. If a person's first name does not positively identify him/her by sex, simply use the complete name in the salutation of the letter (Dear Pat Shiffelbine, for example). If you are addressing the letter to a person only by job title, your salutation may be "Dear Personnel Director." If you are absolutely certain that the personnel director is a man, you may salute him with "Dear Sir" ("Dear Madam" for a woman). The salutation in any business letter should be followed by a colon.

Since you are including something in the envelope besides your letter (your resume and possibly other items), you should indicate at the bottom of the letter that you are enclosing materials. Simply type the word "Enclosure" on the left or right margin near the bottom of the page. If you have enclosed two items along with your letter (resume and college transcript, for example), type "Enclosures (2)." The purpose of this is to let the letter's recipient know that he/she has received everything you sent.

# Contending with Content

What do you say in your cover letter? Typically, a cover letter consists of about four paragraphs: The first one explains why you're writing the letter, the next couple are for tooting your horn and adding information, and the last is for requesting an interview or restating your availability. This format, of course, is not set in stone, and your cover letters may differ considerably from it. You should not, however, write a letter that is so long it does not fit comfortably on one typed page. The sample letters in this chapter should give you a good idea of how yours might serve you. In addition, here's a description of the information most cover letters contain:

*Paragraph 1:*

In your opening paragraph, and probably in your first sentence, explain why you're writing to the employer at this time. Don't make a busy employer wonder for even a few sentences why he's been blessed with a letter from you. If you are "broadcasting" your resumes (that is, sending them out to employers who may not have advertised any openings), simply say that you are writing to inquire about job possibilities with that particular firm or institution. If you are writing in response to an advertised job opening, mention the specific job for which you're applying and say how you found out about it. If your Uncle Fred (or friend Joe or neighbor Inez or anyone else) is employed with the company and told you about the opening, mention his/her name.

Also in this paragraph you can list the items you are enclosing with your letter. Your resume may be your only enclosure, but you also may be sending college transcripts, letters of recommendation, samples of your work (if you're a writer, artist, photographer, etc.), a completed formal application, or some other materials. Listing your enclosures here is in addition to the enclosure notation at the bottom of your letter. You can eliminate confusion by letting the employer know precisely what you're sending.

*Paragraphs 2 and 3:*

One thing you'll probably wish to do in these paragraphs is highlight or elaborate on the items in your resume that especially qualify you for work on this particular job or with this particular firm. This technique allows you to use the same resume throughout your employment search yet stress the most important information for any given job opening. For example, your resume may stress the fact that you earned a business degree in college. It may barely mention that you had a few computer courses. Now you're writing to an employer who has advertised for a business graduate with some computer training. In your cover letter, you can go into some detail about your computer qualifications, and in this way your letter will be an effective complement to your resume.

Or, perhaps you held a job as a radio station copywriter before you got into sales, and your resume entry about that job is rather brief. Now you want to apply for a TV job that will require you to do some copywriting, and you'd like the employer to know more about your copywriting experience. Say it in this section of your cover letter.

And even if your resume stresses the things you'd like stressed, you can still restate those qualifications in your letter. Don't be bashful. Tell the employer why you're right for the job. If some of your qualifications for the job do not, for some reason, appear at all on your resume, this is the place to mention those too.

Another item you may want to include here is a brief explanation of why you'd like to work for this company or institution. Don't fawn at the feet of an employer by telling him that it has been your lifelong dream to labor under his roof, but you *can* mention one or two honest reasons why you'd like to work for him. Perhaps his/her business is the industry (or local) leader in its field. Maybe you just admire the product or service the business produces and will be proud to be associated with it. Maybe the company has a reputation for supporting new research, community involvement, innovative marketing, or some other attribute that is attractive to you. If you can identify why you want to work there, say so.

If nothing concrete comes to mind, skip this item. You should NOT, however, say you'd like to work for the firm because of the high salary, generous vacations, frequent holidays, free insurance coverage, or other fringe benefits it may offer. These things may be (in fact they should be) important to you, but a cover letter is not the place to discuss them.

It may be to your advantage to let the employer know that you have done a bit of specific research on the company. Mention the firm's recent listing as one of the top 100 companies of its kind in the country; or the fact that a new branch has just opened in Houston; or the firm's new internal reorganization; or the just-completed acquisition of a smaller company; or the announcement of a research or production breakthrough; or any other items that will indicate to the employer that you didn't simply choose the company's name out of a phone book.

If you're applying for a job in a distant area and are familiar with the region, you may want to mention that fact. This may be especially important if your job will require you to travel or deal directly with the people of the area (such as a sales position would).

If one or more relatives in your immediate family have been with the company for a long time, you may mention that fact in your cover letter. By itself, this won't get you the job, but some firms do look favorably upon applications by relatives of good employees. If your relative is a valued and trusted worker, the employer's immediate reaction may be to think you might turn out to be the same.

You may want to tell the employer a bit more about yourself in language that might not have seemed appropriate in your resume. You may, in a sentence or two, tell him/her why you'd be good for the firm, what general appealing work characteristics you have, what kind of personality you have, how you approach a new job, or other things about yourself. Just before the sample letters in this chapter you'll find a list of adjectives you might like to use.

You may in your cover letter briefly outline your personal career goals and explain how the job for which you're applying fits into that plan. Before an employer hires you, he/she will want to know where you're headed. If you plan to make a career of the kind of job you're applying for, say so. If you see the firm as one in which you can progress and be fulfilled, say so.

Your present employment may be more important to a prospective new employer than anything else in your resume. If you'd like to elaborate on your current job (or just reemphasize information in your resume), this is the place to do it. In unboastful terms, explain the successes you have had on your present job. If you have been instrumental in increased sales, responsible for innovations, highly commended for your work, or have other feathers in your cap, mention them. The point here is to imply, or even state, that you can be as valuable to your new employer as you are to your present one.

A warning is in order here, however. You should be wary about responding to job advertisements that simply ask you to write to a box number. It just could be that the company to which you're applying IS your present employer—and your boss may be rather unhappy to learn of your wanderlust.

If your employment background or current qualifications are rather unusual, you may wish to briefly explain matters here. If you are in the midst of a career change, your employer may be wondering why a teacher is applying for a position as a computer salesperson, or why a musician wants a job as manager of a clothing store. State your reasons simply and in as few words as possible.

If you are nearly equally qualified in two different areas, it may be to your advantage to point this out to a prospective employer. Let's say you have a double college major, journalism and business, and are applying for a position as a department store manager trainee. Part of the job may involve writing advertising and producing an employee newsletter, and your chances of getting the job will be better if the boss knows you have journalism training as well as a business background.

Finally, you may have a special item of information that should be made known to a prospective employer. If you have a serious handicap (partial or total blindness, severe hearing loss, missing limbs), it is probably a good idea to mention it in your cover letter. It's important, though, to stress that you have overcome this handicap and that it does not seriously impair your ability to do the job (if that is the truth). An employer will learn of your handicap before he/she hires you anyway, so you'll likely be better off mentioning it now. Many employers know from experience that some of their best workers are the determined ones who refuse to let handicaps keep them from doing a good job. Don't go into great detail about your handicap. Just state the facts. And don't list minor things, such as the need for glasses or slight hearing loss, as handicaps.

As with resumes, some items are better left unmentioned in your cover letters. It may be tempting to discuss salaries in your letter, but you should not. At this point, you should be totally concerned with what you can do for the employer, NOT what he/she can do for you. The matter of your salary should not come up until late in your interview, a time when you and the employer can negotiate a mutually agreeable figure. If you're responding to a job advertisement that asks you to state desired salary, you probably will be better off if you use general terms and not dollar amounts. Simply say that salary is "open" or "negotiable" or "to be commensurate with responsibilities" or "to be determined during the interview."

*Paragraph 4:*

This paragraph usually is reserved for action-taking items. As far as you are concerned, of course, the most important action an employer can take is to invite you to an interview. To make this easier for him/her, let the person know when you can be available for such a meeting. If you cannot be available on certain days, by all means say so. But don't restrict the possibilities any more than necessary.

One approach is to invite the employer to call or write you to arrange an interview. A bit bolder technique is to ask if you may call the employer's secretary and schedule yourself for an interview. Of course, the "asking" is a formality, since you don't plan to wait for a response but instead will phone a few days later to get an appointment. The advantage of this more aggressive attack is that it does not require the employer to take any action (other than agreeing to see you when asked by the secretary). The approach you use is up to you. Standard practice is to wait for the employer to request an interview, but if you're the aggressive type you may want to keep the ball in your court and call for an appointment.

Another thing you may want to do in this paragraph is grant your prospective new employer permission to contact your present boss. If your current employer knows you are looking for a job elsewhere and is still likely to speak favorably of you, it might be advantageous to say so in your letter. Formal references will come later, but a quick, informal phone call between employers (who perhaps know each other anyway) may tip the balance in your favor.

If, however, your present employer does not know that you are actively seeking work elsewhere, you should mention this fact in your cover letter and ask the prospective new employer not to contact your present boss at this time. Otherwise, the recipient of your letter may assume it's okay to call your present employer to hear what he/she has to say about you, and your boss may not be too pleased to learn that you're thinking about quitting your job.

Also in this paragraph you can say when you will be available to begin work. If you're a college senior and are sending resumes out in February, you should let prospective employers know that you will not be available to start work until June. Or, if you have any other obligations that will prevent you from starting a new job immediately, let the recipient of your letter know. If your obligations will cause only a short delay, the new employer will probably be willing to accommodate you.

Finally, you can close this paragraph with an optimistic note saying you are eager to talk with the employer and that you look forward to meeting him/her. Thank the employer for considering you for the job. Don't get gushy; just bow out quickly and politely.

# Generally Speaking

Just as with your resume, cover letters should be written in simple, precise, clear English. If you are certain that the person to whom you're writing speaks the technical language of your trade, you surely may use professional jargon in your letter. But many employers and probably most personnel directors are not familiar with all the technical aspects of their companies. If you tell them you designed a completely new version of a D-10 hydraulic feed scanner, they may not know what you're talking about. A detailed description of your technical achievements should be saved for your interview (when you will likely meet a department head or shop foreman). Keep your cover letter language rather general, so it can be understood by anyone reading it.

This does not mean, however, that the language in your cover letters should be so vague that it sounds like a form letter that could be sent to almost any employer. Try to keep the language personal and specific without resorting to jargon.

You also should strive to keep to a minimum the number of times you use the words "I," "me," and "my" in your letters. This may be difficult, because you are, after all, writing about yourself, but letters filled with these personal pronouns can come off sounding a bit presumptuous. Consider this sentence: "I am eager to come to work for your company because I know I can do as good a job for you as I am doing for my present employer." The statement is okay, but "I" appears too often. It would be better if it read: "I am eager to come to work for your company and continue the high quality work I am now doing for XYZ Company."

Or, take a look at this sentence: "I am presently looking for a job in which I will be able to advance as I become more valuable to my employer." A bit wordy and certainly too heavy with personal pronouns. This one is better: "It is important that the job I take offer advancement potential."

# Other Kinds of Letters

Cover letters aren't the only formal messages you may need to write as part of your search for better employment. The others are shorter, sweeter, and not always necessary, but they can be good tools to have at your command. One example of each type of letter appears immediately after the sample cover letters at the end of this section. The format for these letters is the same standard business letter format you'll use for your cover letters. These optional letters are:

FOLLOW-UP/COURTESY LETTER. If your resume and cover letter do their jobs, you will be invited for an interview with the prospective employer. A day or so after that interview, you may wish to send a brief follow-up letter to the person with whom you interviewed. If, in your interview, you forgot to discuss an item or two that may further qualify you for the job, mention them in this letter. If nothing was left out of the interview, simply thank the person again for the opportunity to talk with him/her and reiterate your desire to work for this firm. Few applicants are likely to send such letters, and your courtesy should make a favorable impression on the employer.

ACKNOWLEDGEMENT OF REJECTION LETTER. Alas, you had an interview but were not hired for the job. Don't despair. There are other fish in the employment sea, and the same fish may even bite again. As soon as you've been notified that you will not be hired for the position, you may want to send a short note to the employer. Don't berate him/her for not having the good sense to hire you. Thank him/her for considering you for the job, restate your availability and desire to work for the firm, and ask to be considered for future openings. Here, too, your courtesy will likely make a favorable impression, and you just may get a call the next time an opening pops up.

JOB ACCEPTANCE LETTER. This one will be a pure joy to write. You have been offered the job and are going to take it. You may want to write immediately to the employer restating your eagerness to work for the company, agreeing to the salary offered, and confirming the date you will begin work. This letter, too, is a courtesy, but it also serves to get the salient details of your new employment on paper so there will be no confusion about pay or starting date.

# Presentation and Design

Unlike your resume, which may be photocopied or printed offset, each letter you send in connection with your search for employment must be typed individually. Use only 8½-by-11-inch white bond paper for your letters (unless you have letterhead stationery in a muted color). As with your resume, use a high quality paper with 25 percent or greater cotton (rag) content. Use a good electric typewriter and do (or pay to have done) a first-rate job of typing. A few cleanly corrected mistakes are okay, but if the sheet gets messy, retype it. Don't use the thin, crinkly paper called onionskin, as it lacks heft and dignity. Remember, a potential employer will view this letter as an example of your work. He/she will form a first impression of you based on this letter (and your resume). Do everything you can to make that impression a good one. Finally, if you hire someone to do your typing on a word processor, be sure that person does not justify the right margin (that is, the right margin should not be even like the left one). Your letter should appear as though you typed it yourself on a typewriter, and right margin justification proclaims that it was done some other way.

# Sample Letters

The following sample letters are designed to be used as guides, not as specific models you should adopt word for word. Acceptable variations in format (involving indentation and placement of closing) are used, so you can select a version that appeals to you. No single letter—not the samples and not those you write—should contain all the items mentioned earlier in this section. Include only information that applies to your case and that is important in your job hunt. The first eight samples are cover letters. Each includes a few of the items you may need to put in your cover letters. The last three examples illustrate the other kinds of letters you may wish to write to an employer.

Here's a list of adjectives you may wish to choose from in describing yourself and the work you do:

| | | |
|---|---|---|
| accurate | active | adaptable |
| aggressive | alert | ambitious |
| attentive | broad-minded | conscientious |
| competent | consistent | constructive |
| creative | dependable | determined |
| diplomatic | disciplined | discrete |
| efficient | energetic | enterprising |
| enthusiastic | fair | forceful |
| imaginative | independent | logical |
| loyal | mature | methodical |
| neat | objective | optimistic |
| outgoing | perceptive | personable |
| pleasant | positive | practical |
| precise | productive | proficient |
| realistic | reliable | resourceful |
| respectful | sincere | skilled |
| sophisticated | successful | tactful |

## COVER LETTER

221 Jackson Drive
Hibbing, CO 44556
January 10, 1983


Donna Peterson, Personnel Director
Manville Corporation
Industry Square East
Denver, CO 44589


Dear Ms. Peterson:


I am writing to inquire about possible sales openings with
your firm.  My resume is enclosed.

I am a 1982 graduate of the University of Colorado.  My
major was business administration and my minor psychology.
As my resume indicates, I worked my way through college
selling automobiles full time during the summer and part
time during the school year.  I have acquired an effective
sales technique and have discovered that I work very well in
one-on-one sales situations.

I am a lifelong resident of this part of Colorado and plan
to make my permanent home here.  Eventually, I hope to
become a sales division supervisor with a firm such as
yours.

Do you have any sales openings at this time?  If so, I
would appreciate being considered for a position.  I can be
available for an interview at any time.  I shall look
forward to hearing from you.


Sincerely,


Todd R. Beckwith


Enclosure

## COVER LETTER

919 Cherry St., Apt. #5
Bellview, WA 09870
April 17, 1983


Cecil Roundtree, Manager
Nick's Snack Shop
Highway 10 East
Bellview, WA  09870


Dear Mr. Roundtree:

This letter is in response to your advertisement in the
Bellview Mirror for an assistant manager.  As you requested
in the ad, I am enclosing my resume and two letters of
recommendation.

My resume points out that I have had considerable experience
in the management of small restaurants.  In addition to the
formal employment experience listed on my resume, I grew up
in a family which operated several fast-food restaurants.
While in high school, I assisted my parents in many aspects
of running those businesses.

Presently, I am the second assistant manager of the Eats
Sandwich Shop on Bellview's west side.  I am looking for a
new position with greater responsibility as well as one that
offers an opportunity for advancement.  I would like someday
to become manager of a small restaurant.  Clark Ringgold, my
supervisor at Eats, knows I am looking for a new job.  You may
feel free to call him about me.

I would like very much to talk with you in person about how
I might fit into your organization.  I can arrange to be
available for an interview any afternoon except Fridays.
Thank you for considering me for this position.


Yours very truly,



James Dostado



Enclosures (3)

## COVER LETTER

4560 Blaine St.
Toledo, OH 34387
June 6, 1983


Personnel Director
Hayes Manufacturing Co.
Aberdeen, MI 55569


Dear Personnel Director:


I would like to apply for the position of journeyman machinist as described on your company bulletin board. A friend of mine and an employee of yours, Ned Crockett, told me about the opening. My resume and your company's application form are enclosed.

I am presently self-employed in my own machine shop, but I would like to work for Hayes because of your progressive research and development branch that fully supports new metals technology. Also, frankly, I am looking for a job that offers the potential of long-term employment.

As you can see from my resume, I have had a wide range of experience in working with all types of metals and modern equipment.

It is, I think, only fair to tell you at this time that I am deaf. I am an expert lip reader, however, and my hearing loss does not prevent me in any way from doing an excellent job as a machinist.

I can come to your office for an interview at any time. Thank you for considering me for this job.


Sincerely yours,


Hershel Brady


Enclosures (2)

## COVER LETTER

222 Jefferson Blvd.
Santa Vera, CA 99814
December 4, 1983

Pat Harper, Editor
Today's West Magazine
101 Brooks Avenue
Sunnydale, CA   99670

Dear Editor Harper:

I am applying for the assistant editor position you have advertised in the current edition of Editor magazine. My resume, formal application, portfolio, and two letters of recommendation are enclosed.

As my resume indicates, I have a Master's Degree in journalism, have served as editor of a regional business magazine, and have published dozens of articles in numerous national magazines. I am thoroughly familiar with magazine layout, typesetting, editing techniques, and photography. Also, I have had excellent success in dealing with the occasional conflicts that crop up between editorial and advertising departments on any publication. I am precise, conscientious, and thorough in my work.

I have spent my entire life in the West and enjoy learning about the history, ecology, economics, recreation, and people of the West. I am certain I will be an asset to your publication.

I will be in Sunnydale from December 18 to 22. May I call your secretary and schedule an interview? I look forward to meeting you and to discussing further the contribution I can make to your magazine.

Cordially,

Donald Heffernan

Enclosures (5)

# COVER LETTER

                                            P.O. Box 2456
                                            Phoenix, AZ 98420
                                            February 23, 1983


Nancy Donaldson, Director
Research Division
Starr Oil Company
Petroleum Lane
Houston, TX  11348


Dear Ms. Donaldson:

I wish to apply for any openings you may have in your
oceanographic branch.  My resume and a list of publications
are enclosed.

Although I have spent the last eleven years teaching
mathematics at the university level, it is my desire at this
time to return to the oceanography field.  My masters degree
is in mathematics, and my doctorate is in oceanography.  I
am eager to make this career change, as ocean life has
always been my first love, and scientific research is what I
do best.  As you can see by the material I have published
over the past decade, I have not really been away from these
areas.

My academic credentials should speak for themselves.  Beyond
that, I would like you to know that I am very much a team
player.  I work well with colleagues, and I understand the
structure of large firms such as yours.

I will be in Houston during the last week in March.  I will
call when I arrive and perhaps we can get together for an
initial interview at that time.  If you would like me to
complete a formal application before then, I will be happy
to do so.  I can be available to begin work with your firm
by mid-June.

                                            Sincerely,


                                            Robert F. Lindsay


Enclosures (2)

## COVER LETTER

Apartment #212
Camelot Village
East River Road
Little Lake, WI   34876
April 18, 1983


Dorothy Haskell, Superintendent
Deighton Public Schools
Administration Building
225 E. Lancelot Ave.
Deighton, WI   11221


Dear Ms. Haskell:


I am writing to apply for an elementary teaching position
with your district.  My resume is enclosed, and I have asked
the placement service of the University of Wisconsin to
forward my credentials to you.

As my resume indicates, I have taught second grade for four
years and have always received the highest possible
evaluations.  I am eager to put my experience to work in
your school system.

I can be available for an interview at virtually any time.
Thank you for your consideration.  I'll look forward to
hearing from you.



Sincerely,



Deborah Jenkins



Enclosure

## COVER LETTER

1818 Duncan Drive
Dearborn, OH  44589
October 4, 1983

Delbert Milligan, Manager
Westside Auto Mart
114 West Billings St.
Dearborn, OH    44589

Dear Mr. Milligan:

I am writing to apply for the salesman position you currently have open.  My brother, Jeff Anderson, has been a mechanic at your dealership for nine years.  I learned of the sales opening from him.  My resume is enclosed.

I presently am employed as a salesman for Moffit Enterprises, which distributes personal grooming supplies to retailers throughout the Midwest.  My sales territory includes the entire eastern half of Ohio.  In three years I have increased the number of accounts on that route from 82 to 211 and have tripled sales.  I was named Moffit "Salesman of the Year" in each of those three years.  In my previous job, sales representative for a restaurant supply firm in California, I tripled my sales in just 18 months.  I'm confident I can be as successful at selling automobiles for you as I have been in these sales positions.

My present employer does not know that I am looking for another job, so I must ask that you do not contact anyone at Moffit at this time.

I am almost always in Dearborn on Fridays and Mondays.  Can we schedule an interview on one of those days?  I shall hope to hear from you soon.  Thank you.

Sincerely,

Randall Anderson                                        Enclosure

# COVER LETTER

909 Broomtail Place
Ipswitch, ME   35912
July 10, 1983


Hannah Elfman, President
Bank of Ipswitch
500 Main Street
Ipswitch, ME   35912


Dear Ms. Elfman:


I read with great interest your advertisement for a secretary in the Ipswitch Times.  I would like to apply for that position.  My resume is enclosed.

I believe I am the right person for that job.  I type, take dictation, file, and conduct telephone business as well as anyone you'll ever find.  But beyond those qualifications, I am the "take charge" kind of person your ad said you are looking for.  I can supervise other office workers, arrange office procedures for maximum efficiency, train new help, and in general make your job a lot easier.

I have worked in banks before, and I would be proud to be associated with the Bank of Ipswitch.  I am aware that your bank has consistently been a pioneer in banking innovations as well as in improving employee relations. Your Home Banking Service and your Employee Council are two recent examples of innovations that have impressed me.  In short, I'd like to work for you.

My resume outlines my considerable office experience, and I'd appreciate the opportunity to discuss my qualifications with you in depth.  I can be available for an interview any morning.  I'll look forward to hearing from you.


Yours truly,


Enclosure                                Sally J. Unger

## FOLLOW-UP/COURTESY LETTER

221 S. 4th W.
Kalispell, MT  59874
July 6, 1983


Ed Johnson, Manager
Johnson Bros. Maintenance Services
900 Sapphire Road
Kalispell, MT  59874


Dear Mr. Johnson:


Thank you again for taking the time to visit with me last
Tuesday and for the thorough tour of your facilities.

I think I may have forgotten to mention that I supervise
six employees in my present job, so I am an experienced
foreman.

As you know, I am eager to come to work for Johnson
Brothers.  I shall hope to hear from you soon.


Sincerely,


Ronald Stratton

## ACKNOWLEDGMENT OF REJECTION LETTER

Bellview Court, Number 4
River Road South
Tungston, MS  23098
August 21, 1983


Jennifer Potter, Owner
Jennifer's Fashion Boutique
Northside Mall
Jackson, MS  23581


Dear Ms. Potter:

Thank you for considering me for the sales position.
I enjoyed the tour of your boutique.

I was disappointed to learn that I was not chosen for
the job, but I know you had many qualified applicants from
which to choose.  I would appreciate it if you could keep
my resume on file so that I might be considered for future
openings.

Thank you.


                              Cordially yours,



                              Shelly Biderhold

## JOB ACCEPTANCE LETTER

409 Plankton Place
Galveston, TX  09245
September 4, 1983


Daniel Weber, Manager
Marine Technologies, Inc.
10 Pier Avenue West
Galveston, TX  09246


Dear Mr. Weber:


Thank you very much for offering me the position of diving
supervisor.  I am eager to come to work for you, and I will
be able to begin October 1, as you suggested.  Your salary
offer of $31,000 is acceptable as well.

I'm looking forward to instituting some of the changes we
talked about during my interview.  Again, thank you.


Yours truly,


James Batson

# Chapter 6

# SAMPLE RESUMES

The following resumes are provided as examples to guide you in the preparation of your own top quality resume. You should not appropriate complete sections for use in your document, because the words you use must describe your situation and yours only. I suggest that you skim through these resumes to find one that appeals to your eye and then follow that format, underlining, capitalization, etc., in preparing your resume.

Then, you'll likely wish to read many of these resumes in their entirety to get a solid feeling for the kind of language you're going to be using. If you run across specific words or phrases that may work well in your resume, mark them for later reference. Immerse yourself in resume style, so that when you begin to compose your resume, its construction will seem almost second nature to you.

Chronological resumes are first; you'll recognize them by the prominent way the dates are displayed. Then come several functional resumes; these generally have specific skill areas highlighted. Finally, a few creative resumes are provided for your perusal; remember to think twice and then three times before using a creative resume, as they usually miss the mark.

Try to find a resume style that (1) does a good job of imparting information to a reader and (2) makes you feel good about having your name at the top of the page. If you follow the guidelines discussed earlier in this book and pattern your resume after the samples appearing here, that better job should soon be yours.

## INSURANCE AGENT

WILLIAM F. CHARBONEAU

45 Baywood Lane
Portland, OR  66573
Telephone: 505-887-9087

Professional Objective

To become manager of my own insurance company.

Insurance Experience

1980 to present     Agent, Cris Caldwell Insurance Agency, Portland, OR.  Write and service life, health, home, and auto policies for individuals.  Deal with 11 different insurance companies.  Am consistently top-selling agent in the agency.  Have received merits awards four times in three years.

1977 to 1980     Agent, Toole and Tufington Insurance Agency, Medford, OR.  Primarily handled group health policies for large employers.  Achieved high success rate making cold contacts throughout Oregon.

1975 to 1977     Agent, Iverson and Associates, Beaverton, OR.  Worked mostly with government employees in setting up annuities.  Made large and small group presentations to teachers as well as to state, county, and city workers.  Increased firm's annuity trade 150 percent in three years.

Management Experience

1970 to 1974     Manager, Safeway Food Store, Missoula, MT.  Supervised 19 employees.  Prepared work schedules, hired and fired, and made all other management decisions for store doing more than $700,000 in business annually.  Twice elected city Retailer of the Year.

                        WILLIAM F. CHARBONEAU


1968 to 1970        Partner and Manager, Brooks Street
                    Appliance Store, Missoula, MT.  Sold
                    washers, dryers, and other large
                    appliances.  Employed six workers.
                    Performed all management duties relative
                    to small retail operation.


                              Education

1975                Hartford Insurance Institute, Hartford,
                    CT.  Six-week course covering all phases
                    of insurance business.

1965 to 1969        University of Montana, Missoula, MT.
                    B.A. Degree in business administration.
                    Graduated with honors.


                               General

Am affable, hard-working businessman.  Enjoy challenges and
meeting new people.  Am comfortable in supervisory role.
Would like to take over local insurance agency affiliated
with one major national insurer.


                              Personal

               Born:  December 9, 1947
                  Health:  Excellent
         Marital Status:  Married; three children
               Residence:  Own home
                   Am bondable


                             References

                    Available on request.

# LIBRARIAN
---

HAZEL HOOD


4415 Empire Street
Los Angeles, CA 90908
Telephone: 818-444-6908


LIBRARIAN


## Experience

1977 to present     Research Librarian, Los Angeles County
                    Library, Los Angeles, CA.  Supervise
                    three assistants.  Research topics as
                    requested.  Frequently work with local
                    law enforcement agencies in doing legal
                    research.  Perform searches at request of
                    libraries across country.  Conduct
                    computer and traditional searches.

1972 to 1975        Children's Librarian, Sacramento Public
                    Library, Sacramento, CA.  Managed entire
                    children's section.  Supervised two other
                    librarians.  Devised programs that led to
                    80 percent increase in use of library by
                    children.  Worked closely with local
                    teachers in coordinating reading programs.

1970 to 1972        Reference Librarian, Watertown, SD,
                    Municipal Library.  Assisted patrons with
                    general reference problems.  Gave tours
                    of library.  Spoke to school classes.
                    Performed wide range of general librarian
                    duties.


## Education

1975 to 1977        Sacramento State College, Sacramento,
                    CA.  M.A. Degree in library science.
                    3.9 GPA.  Received Belton Award for
                    outstanding achievement in library work.
                    Wrote thesis on development of library
                    technology.

HAZEL HOOD


1966 to 1970          Northern State College, Aberdeen, SD.
                      B.S. Degree in library science.  On
                      dean's list six out of eight semesters.
                      Member Sigma Tau Delta honorary
                      fraternity.


Publications

"Ten Steps Toward Better Children's Sections," May, 1973,
Journal of Library Science.

"Caper's for Kids," August, 1973, Library magazine.

"The Computer is Coming," July, 1978, Library Today.

"Using Computer Data Banks in Library Research," April,
1980, Journal of Library Science.


Personal

                      Born:  May 4, 1948
                      Health:  Excellent
                      Marital Status:  Married
                      Location Preference:  Prefer Los Angeles area


References

          Available upon request.

# RETAILER (PHOTO)

DAVID GRANLEY
114 N. State Street
Elkton, ME 12345
Telephone: 502-221-6701

Occupational
 Objective          Position in retail photographic sales.

Experience

3/80 to present     The Photo Shop, Elkton, ME.  Firm is
                    photo specialty store.  Sells photographic
                    supplies and services.  Counsels customers
                    in appropriate selection of equipment.
                    Handles customer complaints.  Processes
                    and prints black and white film.  Assists
                    with stocking, inventory, and display.

4/79 to 3/80        Sears, Portland, ME.  Sold photo and
                    stereo equipment.  Functioned as manager
                    in supervisor's absence.  Responsible for
                    cash register balance at end of day.  Set
                    up store displays and assisted customers
                    with home installation of sound equipment.
                    Was consistently the department's top
                    salesman.

8/76 to 2/78        Jackson's Drug Store, Portland, ME.
                    Operated cash register, assisted customers
                    with non-drug purchases, and conducted
                    inventory.

Education

1975 to 1976        University of Maine, Portland, ME.
                    Journalism major.  Took photos for school
                    newspaper.  Worked part-time as freelance
                    photographer for Portland Crier newspaper.

1970 to 1974        Hawthorne High School, Portland, ME.
                    Active in speech and debate.  Took photos
                    for yearbook and school newspaper.

## DAVID GRANLEY

General                 Skilled in most aspects of photography
                        and the processing of black and white
                        film.  Has done wedding photography and
                        worked with models.  General knowledge of
                        photographic paper and chemicals.
                        Complete knowledge of cameras and
                        accessories.  Is aggressive salesman and
                        reliable employee.


Personal                Born:  August 6, 1956
                        Health:  Excellent
                        Appearance: height 5'10"; weight 170 lbs.
                        Marital Status: Single
                        Location Preference:  Willing to relocate


References
   and                  Available on request.
Portfolio

# MANAGER (INDUSTRY)

ROBERT FISHER

2109 Pinchon Street
Rochester, NY  10556                    Telephone: 212-334-6781

## Professional Objective

Position in industrial management.

## Experience

Lockwood Aeronautics, Inc., Rochester, NY. 1970 to 1982.
Firm manufactures small and mid-size aircraft.  At various
times held positions of general manager, secretary-treasurer,
and president.  Performed following duties:

Finance: Negotiated and secured corporate loans
in excess of $50 million.  Procured customer loan
requirements, arranged long-term expansion
financing, and projected money requirements.

Acquisitions:  Purchased land for plant expansion.
Assisted with new plant design and awarded
construction contracts.  Also acquired subsidiary
company.

Legal:  Served as primary legal liaison.  Assisted
in several litigations.  Prepared bills for
introduction in state legislature.  Administered
regulations for numerous federal programs.

Accounting:  Assumed responsibility for all
accounting functions and related internal controls.
Purchased computers and assisted in development of
software.  Served as liaison to corporate and
federal auditors.

Personnel:  Staffed new plant and regularly oversaw
activities of 450-500 employees.

Halverson's Department Store, Scotio, NY. 1967 to 1970.
Managed store consisting of 14 departments and employing
32 workers.

ROBERT FISHER

Landers Construction Co., Landers, NY. 1965 to 1967.
Kept books and performed all accounting functions.

## Education

New York State University, Ipswitch, NY.   1958 to 1962.
B.A. Degree in business.

## Military

U.S. Army. 1962 to 1964.
Served in Korea.  Achieved rank of major.  Handled supply
logistics for 600-man post.  Honorable discharge.

## Affiliations

Rotary Club
American Legion
Kiwanis International
Association of Corporate Presidents
New York State University Advisory Board

## References

Available on request.

## TRAVEL AGENT

BEVERLY SUSKIND

2909 Bancroft Avenue
Dallas, TX  89723
Telephone: 909-888-2351

### Occupational Objective

Employment as travel agent.

### Experience

Ticket Agent, American Airlines, Dallas, TX.  Counseled
customers, wrote tickets, checked bags, and resolved
complaints in busy airport setting.  Became thoroughly
familiar with airline schedules and ticketing procedures.
1980 to present.

Flight Attendant, Republic Airlines, Dallas, TX.  Performed
all flight attendant duties on domestic flights throughout
Midwest.  1977 to 1980.

Employment Counselor, Gateway Employment Agency, Houston, TX.
Worked one-on-one with clients to secure employment.
Achieved 77 percent success record.  Worked closely with
employers to match worker with job.  Became familiar with
computer data storage and retrieval techniques.  1976 to
1977.

Personal Travel.  Traveled extensively throughout Europe
with military father.  Attended local schools in France and
Germany.  Became very familiar with western Europe.
Acquainted with rail and air travel procedures in most
European nations.  1963 to 1972.

### Education

University of Texas, Austin, TX.  Drama major.  Appeared in
several major theater performances.  1973 to 1975.

### Personal

Born:  March 6, 1955
Health:  Excellent
Single
Willing to relocate
Speak French, German,
and some Spanish

### References

Available on request.

## SCHOOL PRINCIPAL

HOWARD BURTON

456 Dixon Street                     Work Phone: 404-789-9023
Lakeview, WA 87659                   Home Phone: 404-445-7321


Position Desired:    High school principal.

Experience:     Serves as principal in high school of
                750 students.  Cut truancy rate by 90
                percent.  Reduced annual teacher turnover
                rate from 50 percent to 10 percent.
                Instituted back to basics curriculum.
                1978 to present.  Lakeview High School,
                Lakeview, WA.

                Assistant Principal in 1200-student junior
                high school.  Evaluated teachers, revised
                curriculum, wrote grant applications, and
                was in charge of student discipline.
                Created incentive program that decreased
                absences 15 percent.  1975 to 1978.
                Bellingham Junior High, Bellingham, WA.

                Teacher of math and science, several
                different high schools.  1965 to 1975.

Education:      Master of Education Degree, University of
                Washington, Pullman, WA.  Administration
                major.  Graduated 1975.

                B.S. Degree in Education, University of
                Colorado, Denver, CO.  Math major.  General
                science minor.  Graduated 1965.

Affiliations:   Washington Education Association
                National Education Association
                American Teachers of Math
                U.S. Association of Secondary Principals

Personal:       Health:  Excellent
                Married
                Willing to relocate

References:     Available on request and from Universities
                of Colorado and Washington.

# POLICE OFFICER

JESSE WEBER

7765 Bordeau Drive
San Antonio, TX  44456

## Employment Objective

Position as uniformed police officer.

## Experience

1980 to present      POLICE OFFICER, Midland, TX.  Directed
                     traffic, controlled crowds, patroled
                     on foot and in squad car, visited schools,
                     investigated crimes and accidents, and
                     accomplished other general law
                     enforcement duties in city of 33,000.
                     Cited twice by City Council for
                     outstanding achievement.

1974 to 1979         MILITARY POLICEMAN, U.S. Air Force.
                     Served in Thailand and on several
                     U.S. bases.

## Education and Training

1979 to 1980         TEXAS POLICE ACADEMY, Austin, TX.
                     Completed all requirements of academy.
                     Learned firearm use, guard dog handling,
                     riot control, self-defense, and crime
                     investigation.  Honor graduate.

1970 to 1974         LOVELAND HIGH SCHOOL, Loveland, TX.
                     Graduated 1974.

## Personal

Born:  January 4, 1956        Health:  Excellent
Height:  Six feet             Weight:  180 pounds
Will relocate                 Single

## References

Available on request

## TAX PREPARER

MELVIN STROFUS

#6, Highline Court
Appelton, WI  23541                        Phone: 303-999-8723

Objective:         Part-time position as preparer of federal
                   and state income tax returns.


Tax Experience:

                   Prepared tax returns for P & I, Inc.; Tax
                   Associates Inc.; Happy Returns Inc.; and
                   several regional accounting firms.
                   Employed generally from January through
                   April.  Worked unsupervised in
                   preparation of individual, proprietorship,
                   partnership, and (small) corporate returns.
                   No client has ever had to pay penalty.
                   Became thoroughly familiar with federal
                   and Wisconsin tax laws.  1974 to present.

     Other
Qualifications:    * Am knowledgeable about current tax laws
                   * Can work long hours during rush months
                   * Need no supervision
                   * Have own commercial calculator
                   * Know how to get all legal deductions
                   * Relate well to customers


Education:         University of Wisconsin.  Three years as
                   business major.


Personal:          Excellent health
                   Single
                   Able to work nights


References:        Available on request.

## DENTAL ASSISTANT

RUTH ANN SNIVELY

515 Beckwith Street
Lincoln, NB  22356                    Telephone:  908-777-5612

<u>Dental Assistant</u>

GOAL:             Employment as assistant for an established
                  dentist in a Nebraskan urban area.

EXPERIENCE:

1979 to 1982      DAVID GRAY, dentist, Lincoln, NB.  Assisted
                  with all routine dental procedures as well
                  as with minor oral surgery.  Kept
                  appointment and payment records.  Devised
                  plan for automatic mailing of check-up
                  promptings.

1976 to 1979      WANGER AND WINSHIP, dentists, Omaha, NB.
                  Assisted with all dental procedures.  Also
                  taught patients dental hygiene practices.

1975              TERRANCE ZIMM, dentist, Omaha, NB.  Six-month
                  internship for vocational school.  Became
                  familiar with dental office practices,
                  on-the-job use of tools and equipment, and
                  customer relations.

EDUCATION:

1973 to 1975      SIOUX CENTER VOCATIONAL SCHOOL, Omaha, NB.
                  Completed dental assistant program with "B"
                  average.

1969 to 1973      WASHINGTON HIGH SCHOOL, Omaha, NB.

PERSONAL:         Born:  August 11, 1951
                  Health:  Excellent
                  Marital Status:  Single
                  Willing to relocate

REFERENCES:       Available from Placement Office, Sioux Center
                  Vocational School, 100 S. Russell Street,
                  Omaha, NB 22355.  Additional references
                  available upon request.

# PRODUCTION WORKER

Julio Stephano


1107 Roland Way
Detroit, MI  69633
Telephone:  505-987-6670


Objective:  Employment as factory production worker.


Experience:

1978 to present    Assembly worker, National Motor Co.,
                   Detroit, MI.  Assembled housings in
                   transmission division.  Missed only three
                   days of work in five years.

1974 to 1978       Production worker, Tompson Plastics Inc.,
                   Gary, IN.  Inspected and fitted plastic
                   components in toy department.  Consistently
                   received highest possible work ratings.

1961 to 1974       Solder line worker, Teko Electronics,
                   Chicago, IL.  Soldered circuitry in a
                   variety of electrical appliances.
                   Compiled excellent work record.


Education:

1956 to 1960       Denton High School, Cicero, IL.
                   Graduated 1960.


Personal:

Excellent health                        Will relocate
Married; three children                 Speak Spanish


References:

              Available on request.

## BIOLOGIST
JULIE BARRYMAN

P.O. Box 2250
Sherman, MS 20205
Phone: (708) 455-7813

Employment Goal:  Position as staff biologist with federal
                  or state agency.

Experience:       BIOLOGIST, Texas Department of Fish and
                  Wildlife.  Assisted with studies of several
                  species of game animals and fish.
                  Participated in game management decisions.
                  Prepared biological specimens as evidence in
                  court.  Taught wildlife biology refresher
                  classes to department law enforcement
                  personnel.  Conducted in-depth study of
                  black bass.  1979 to 1983.

                  BIOLOGIST, National Park Service.  Employed
                  primarily as naturalist at Yellowstone
                  National Park, WY.  Conducted a variety of
                  interpretive programs for visitors on park
                  flora and fauna.  Performed winter big game
                  species inventory.  Wrote appraisals of park
                  management policies.  Became very familiar
                  with public relations techniques and with
                  bureaucratic structures.  1976 to 1979.

                  BIOLOGY CONSULTANT, Texaco Oil Company,
                  Baton Rouge, LA.  Advised firm about
                  biological considerations relating to oil
                  production in wetlands.  Wrote environmental
                  impact statements.  Helped company earn
                  national award as conservation-minded
                  industry.  1974 to 1976.

Education:        M.S. Degree in ecosystem biology, University
                  of Colorado, Denver, CO.  Wrote thesis on
                  marsh ecosystem.  Earned National Wildlife

## JULIE BARRYMAN

Federation Conservation Award.  Lobbied
Colorado legislature for wetland protection
laws.  Graduated 1974.

B.S. Degree in biology, University of
Montana, Missoula, MT.  3.7 GPA.  Member
Wildlife Club.  Graduated 1973.

Affiliations:  International Assoc. of Wildlife Biologists
American Assoc. of Wildlife Biologists
Federation of Park Naturalists
Institute for Wetlands Preservation (director)

Personal:       Born: Oct. 10, 1950
Health:  Good
Willing to relocate
Willing to work out of remote sites

References:     Available on request.

# AUTOMOTIVE MECHANIC

NORMAN STICKLER

2192 Central Avenue West
Columbus, VT 21082
Telephone: 414-342-5692

## Occupational Objective

Position as an apprentice foreign car mechanic.

## Experience Highlights

1980 - 1982    BINGHAM VOLKSWAGEN, Columbus, VT.  Prepared
used cars for resale.  Tuned engines,
repaired brakes, checked cooling systems, and
performed troubleshooting on electrical
systems.  Worked under guidance of
journeyman mechanic.  Occasionally assisted
with warranty repair on new VWs.

1979 - 1980    SKIFTON HONDA, Columbus, VT.  Assisted with
broad range of four-cylinder engine repair,
specializing in cooling systems and brakes.
Received "Employee of Month" award twice.

1978 - 1979    TURNER'S TEXACO, Columbus, VT.  Installed
shock absorbers, mufflers, and tires.  Tuned
engines.  Diagnosed engine trouble.

## Education

1981           Dunraven Tune-Up School, Glouster, VT.
Four-week technical course dealing exclusively
with small auto engines.

1979           Texaco Technical Training School, Hanibal,
VT.  Two weeks.  General auto repair course.

1974 - 1978    Colonial High School. Columbus, VT.  Took
several metal shop, wood shop, and auto
mechanics classes.  Graduated 1978.

NORMAN STICKLER

## General

Wish to become journeyman mechanic.  Looking for a career as well as a job.  Take pride in work and know when to ask questions.

## Personal

| | |
|---|---|
| Born | September 1, 1960 |
| Health | Excellent |
| Marital Status | Married; one child |
| Interests | Hunting, reading, firearms, bowling |

## References

Available on request.

## CONSTRUCTION WORKER

DAVID BLASINGAME

4215 West Fifth Street                    Born: November 10, 1934
Ogden, UT 56987                           Health: Excellent
Phone: 804-989-8765                       Willing to relocate


OBJECTIVE          Full-time employment in construction trade.


WORK RECORD

1978 to 1981       Foreman, Far West Contractors, Inc.,
                   Ogden, UT.  Supervised construction crews
                   and coordinated subcontractors' work on
                   commercial and industrial building projects.
                   Personally assisted with tasks ranging from
                   design to finish work.  Became thoroughly
                   familiar with large project construction.

1973 to 1978       Partner, Ferny Construction Co., Ferny,
                   UT.  Built and remodeled homes.  Performed
                   all work except plumbing and wiring.
                   Employed three workers.

1964 to 1973       Foreman, Andrews Construction Co.,
                   Bellingham, WA.  Began as carpenter and
                   later promoted to foreman.  Built all types
                   of small commercial structures.  Learned
                   techniques of construction.


EDUCATION

1962 to 1964       Carpenter Apprentice School, Bellingham, WA.

1954 to 1958       Lincoln High School, Bellingham, WA.


MILITARY

1958 to 1962       U.S. Navy.  Honorable discharge.


PERSONAL

Good health....Will relocate....Married....Have own tools.

## SALESPERSON

SANDRA R. GOODHEART

2342 Hillborough Heights
Raleigh, NC 34521
Telephone: 342-783-2236

## Occupational Objective

Position in sales or sales management with firm dealing in business communications equipment or business security devices.

## Experience Highlights

1978 - 1982     Commudata Inc., Atlanta, GA.  Firm makes and sells electronic data transferral and communications devices for small businesses.

Began primarily as field representative for solicitation of new accounts in 4 eastern states.  Made cold contacts and demonstrated equipment.  Became adept at closing sales after initial demonstration.  Consistently one of firm's top three salespersons (out of nearly 50).

Promoted to sales supervisor for North and South Carolina.  Oversaw work of 9 salesmen who wrote orders for about 34 percent of firm's total business while covering only 20 percent of total area.

1974 - 1978     Security Systems Inc., Atlanta, GA.  Sold electronic security systems to commercial and residential customers.  Served as sole representative for all of Florida.  Made cold contacts and assisted with system installations.  Received numerous company awards for salesmanship.

## SANDRA R. GOODHEART

### Education

1972 - 1973    University of North Florida, Jacksonville,
               FL.  Business major.

1968 - 1972    Green Cove High School, Green Cove
               Springs, FL.  Graduated 1972.

### Personal

Single
In excellent health
Willing to relocate
Willing to travel extensively

### References

Available on request

# BUSINESSPERSON

ANDREA BILLINGSLY


719 Pine Street
Yorba Linda, CA 90823
Telephone: 909-568-4343


Resume Summary      Familiar with small business operation,
                    office management, and sales.


Experience

10/80 to present    Office Manager, Coastal Insurance
                    Company, Yorba Linda, CA.  Prepares
                    insurance contracts, designs advertising,
                    keeps books, computes payroll, conducts
                    correspondence, and performs other
                    general office work.


4/78 to 9/80        Saleswoman, Van Gotten's Department
                    Store, San Diego, CA.  Floated among all
                    women's departments.  Repeatedly
                    commended for sales record.


5/76 to 4/78        Loan Processor, General Motors
                    Acceptance Corp., San Diego, CA.  Began
                    as credit investigator and then promoted
                    to loan department.  Wrote loan
                    contracts.  Entered data in computer.
                    Compiled monthly reports.


2/71 to 2/76        Partner, Ruby's Beauty Salon, San Diego,
                    CA.  Worked full-time as co-manager.
                    Employed six beauticians.  Hired and
                    fired, devised promotions, kept books,
                    computed payroll and taxes, and dealt
                    personally with customers.


Education

1968 to 1970        Valley Community College, San Diego, CA.
                    Completed two-year program in accounting
                    and business management.  Extensive
                    training in practical aspects of small
                    business operation.

ANDREA BILLINGSLY

1964 to 1968            Bayshore High School, San Diego, CA.
                        Graduated near top of class of 400.
                        Took all available clerical and
                        business classes.


Personal

Born:                   August 14, 1950
Health:                 Good
Appearance:             Height 5'5"; Weight 118 pounds
Marital Status:         Single
Residence:              Owns home
Travel:                 Willing to do extensive travel
Location:               Willing to relocate anywhere in West
Language:               Speak some Spanish
Interests:              Scuba diving, sailing, photography


References:             Available on request.

## MARKET RESEARCHER

WANDA TERRAULT

2121 N. Birchwood
Memphis, TN  90123
Phone: 202-876-2301

Occupational Objective

Position in marketing or public relations.

Experience

2/80 to present     MANAGER, Trim 'N' Slim Weight Loss
                    Salon, Memphis, TN.  Plans, directs,
                    controls, and coordinates activities of
                    salon.  Supervises six employees.
                    Responsible for customer services,
                    program and product sales, payments,
                    advertising, and financial reports.
                    Has increased sales 45 percent in two
                    years.

10/76 to 12/79      SALESPERSON, Miss Marge's, Memphis, TN.
                    Firm is retail women's clothing store.
                    Sold apparel, assisted with display,
                    compiled financial reports, and conducted
                    marketing research.  Also handled large
                    amounts of money.  Part-time while
                    attending university.

3/75 to 9/76        DIRECTOR OF RECREATION, Dawson, TN.
                    Developed and coordinated recreational
                    programs for all ages.  Conducted
                    research to assess community's recreation
                    needs.  Hired and supervised four other
                    employees.

6/73 to 2/75        ASSISTANT MANAGER, The Devil Dancer,
                    Wichita, KS.  Firm deals in Indian
                    artifacts.  Assisted owners in all
                    phases of retail operation including
                    display, advertising, budgeting,
                    bookkeeping, and purchasing.

WANDA TERRAULT

## Education

1976 to 1979          MEMPHIS STATE UNIVERSITY, Memphis, TN.
                      B.A. Degree in management and marketing.
                      Graduated with honors.  Member Alpha
                      Delta Mu scholastic honorary fraternity.
                      Received $500 scholarship from U.S.
                      Chamber of Commerce.

## Volunteer Work

Red Cross
United Way
Heart Fund
Big Brothers and Sisters
Asian Refugee Assistance Group

## Personal

Health:  Excellent.........Single.........Will relocate

## References

Available on request.

## MANAGER (AUTO)

RON LEAVEY
River Gate Road, Box 112
Bismarck, ND  54360
Phone: 404-231-9824

### Occupational Objective

Management position in automotive business.

### Experience

1980 - 1982     Mechanic, Tune-Up Center, Bismarck, ND.
Performed all tune-up operations and acted as
manager in owner's frequent absence.  Opened
and closed shop, scheduled appointments,
handled receipts, diagnosed mechanical
problems, and sold needed repairs.

1979 - 1980     Service Manager, North Country Ford,
Bismarck, ND.  Assisted in planning new plant
and establishing service department for three
makes of cars.  Supervised nine other
employees.  Administered successful direct
mail, newspaper, and radio advertising
programs.  Instituted incentive pay programs.
Constantly attempted to motivate employees to
have pride in their work and a caring
attitude toward customers.

1974 - 1979     Service Manager, Nordak Imports, Bismarck, ND.
Firm sold Datsun and Mercedes automobiles.
Helped plan new building and organize service
department.  Supervised 14 employees.
Introduced the "team" concept of auto service,
which gives responsibility and credit to
mechanics.

Also assisted with financial aspects of the
business.  Analyzed profit and loss reports
as well as yearly projections for labor,
sales, and parts.  In owner's absence, signed
payroll checks, dealt with manufacturers, and
resolved customer complaints.

1968 - 1973     Service Manager, Dennison Honda, Fargo, ND.
Performed all duties of service manager.
Began as mechanic and later promoted.

RON LEAVEY

1963 - 1968          Mechanic, Import Motors, Santa Barbara, CA.
                     Performed full range of auto mechanic duties.


## Education and Training

1978                 Mercedes Benz Management Seminar.  Learned
                     service management, financial statement,
                     motivational, and customer contact skills.

1975, 1976           Datsun Management Seminars.  Learned
                     management skills.

1956 - 1959          Central High School, Indianapolis, IN.
                     Graduated 1959.


## Military

U.S. Air Force.  Served as aircraft mechanic.  Honorable
discharge.


## General

Work well with people.  Am adept at solving customer and
personnel complaints.  Enjoy motivating people and assuring
smooth operation of business.


## Personal

Health:  Excellent
Born:  March 22, 1942
Residence:  Own home
Travel: Willing to do some travel
Marital Status:  Married; two children
Appearance:  Height 6'1"; Weight 165 lbs.
Interests:  Hunting, snowmobiling, camping, fishing


## References

Available upon request.

## BUSINESS ADMINISTRATOR

BARBARA WINTERS

1002 Winston Ave. N.W.
St. Paul, MN
(509) 251-3581

Resume Capsule

Thoroughly familiar with institutional administration,
personnel procedures, counseling, and small business
operation.

Experience

12/80 - 5/82    Education Director, Canby, MN. Worked with
local school district in coordinating school
and community activities, securing federal
and state grants, and developing a program to
combat truancy and delinquency. Supervised
staff of four. Prepared budget, recruited
employees, and served as general liaison
between school and community.

4/78 - 8/80    Owner, J.B. Bookstore, Rochester, MN.
Employed three clerks. Doubled sales of
previous owner. Managed all aspects of small
business operation.

1/75 - 2/78    Training Director, United Way of St. Paul,
St. Paul, MN. Developed personnel training
policies for charity employing 150 workers.
Prepared budgets, designed affirmative action
plans, wrote job descriptions, recruited, and
produced audiovisual training materials.

9/71 - 11/74    Counselor, Minnesota Home for Unwed Mothers,
Fairbush, MN. Advised young mothers about
legal rights, employment skills, and work
habits. Conducted group and individual
counseling for unmarried mothers who were
about to leave the institution. Assisted 88
percent of these women in finding jobs.

## BARBARA WINTERS

### Education

1969 - 1971    University of Minnesota, St. Paul, MN.
               M.A. Degree in Counseling, 3.8 GPA.

1965 - 1969    Mankato State College, Mankato, MN.
               B.S. Degree.  Business Administration major.
               Sociology minor.

### Affiliations

National Association of Counselors
Minnesota Society of School Administrators
National Federation of Teachers
Minnesota Federation of Teachers

### Personal

Born: March 21, 1946
Marital Status: Married
Health: Excellent

### References

Available on request.

## MANAGER/SALESPERSON

BART J. GOEFFINA
7814 Hillview Way
San Francisco, CA 98012

OCCUPATIONAL HISTORY

Dates.............................................1978 to Present
Location.....................................San Francisco, CA
Firm.........................Jackson and Associates Rentals
Position.................Manager of Apartment Rental Units
Duties:  Collects rents, places ads, arranges for repairs,
         evicts tenants, keeps books, and oversees other
         aspects of more than 100 rental units.


Dates...............................................1971 to 1978
Location.....................................San Francisco, CA
Firm...................................West Winds Family Motel
Position.........................................Owner/Manager
Duties:  Managed all facets of operation of 52-unit motel.
         Employed 2-4 workers.


Dates...............................................1963 to 1971
Location...........................................Medford, OR
Firm.............................................Red Carpet Realty
Position..............................................Salesman
Duties:  Sold residential and commercial real estate.


Dates...............................................1960 to 1963
Location...........................................Medford, OR
Firm............................State Farm Insurance Company
Position..............................................Salesman
Duties:  Sold life, health, home and auto insurance to
         individuals and businesses.


EDUCATION

UNIVERSITY OF OREGON, Portland, OR.  B.A. Degree in Business
Administration.  Psychology minor.  1956 to 1960.


MILITARY

U.S. ARMY.  Served in Korea and in Germany as communications
supervisor.  Honorable discharge.  1948 to 1956.

## BART J. GOEFFINA

### GENERAL

Has complete knowledge of small business operation.  Is
efficient manager of employees.  Works well with all types
of people.

### PERSONAL

```
Born.............................................April 4, 1930
Health.................,...................................Good
Residence............................................Owns Home
Marital Status................Married; three adult children
Interests.........................Bowling, golf, racketball
```

### REFERENCES

Available on request.

## HOSPITAL DIRECTOR

MARGARET F. HASTINGS


219 Balboa Drive
Santa Cruz, CA  90823
(213) 666-7801


## Occupational Objective

Position as director of hospital mental health unit.


## Education

1980 to present    University of California, Santa Cruz
                   Branch, CA.  Pursuing B.S. Degree in
                   nursing.  Part-time.  Expects to complete
                   program in 1983.

1970 to 1972       Northern Ohio University, Lansing, OH.
                   Earned Associate Degree in registered
                   nursing.  Took clinical training at
                   Mayo Clinic.


## Experience

4/78 to present    Santa Cruz Community Hospital, Santa
                   Cruz, CA.  Staff nurse.  Works night
                   shift while attending school days.
                   Conducts group therapy.  Serves as charge
                   nurse on weekends.

1/77 to 3/78       Clay County Memorial Hospital, Santa
                   Cruz, CA.  Staff nurse.  Served in
                   intensive care and coronary care units.

2/74 to 12/76      Cedars Hospital, Oak Park, CA.  Served
                   as team leader and charge nurse.  Worked
                   in adolescent treatment program.
                   Occasionally functioned as charge nurse,
                   scheduling staff of 36 employees.  Led
                   group sessions.  Conducted team meetings.
                   Combined physicians' directives with staff
                   opinions in development of treatment
                   plan for each patient.

## MARGARET F. HASTINGS

6/72 to 2/74        Lansing General Hospital, Lansing, OH.
                    Charge nurse.  Worked primarily in
                    psychiatric ward.


### General

Has done volunteer work with troubled adolescents.  Was
active in group seeking to establish chapter of Mental
Health Association.  Would be willing as director to work
flexible hours in order to maintain continuous open
communications with staff.


### References

Available upon request.

# FLIGHT ATTENDANT

LINDA JOHANSSON

812 Ronan Drive, Apt. 6
Tacoma, WA  80215
(325) 667-9812

## EMPLOYMENT OBJECTIVE

Position as airline flight attendant.

## WORK HISTORY

6/80 to 3/83:    Chalet Supper Club, Tacoma, WA.  Served as hostess, bartender, and cocktail waitress. Closed out cash register and took responsibility for large sums of money. Received two pay raises and one promotion in first year.

4/77 to 4/78:    Dandy Don's Dinner Club, Seattle, WA. Began as waitress and later promoted to chief hostess.  Learned how to greet customers and see that their needs were met.

6/76 to 2/77:    Barclay Insurance Co., Seattle, WA. Receptionist.  Also performed some general office duties.

## EDUCATION

1974 to 1976:    Seattle Community College, Seattle, WA. Took general course of studies.

1970 to 1974:    Ocean View High School, Seattle, WA. Graduated 1974.

## GENERAL

Have friendly, outgoing personality.  Enjoy meeting and assisting new people.  Have good math and mechanical aptitudes. Like to travel.  Am confident of ability to represent an airline as flight attendant and to uphold firm's public image.

LINDA JOHANSSON

## PERSONAL

Born:  1956                          Health:  Excellent
Height:  5'5"                        Weight:  127 pounds
Marital Status:  Single              Speak some French
Eager to travel                      Willing to relocate


## REFERENCES

Available on request.

## CONSTRUCTION WORKER

BILL BRADFORD

511 East Broadway
Billings, MT 59800
406-331-6401

### Objective

Employment in construction trade.

### Education

1979 to 1983      Billings Central High School, Billings, MT.
Graduated 1983.  Maintained "B" average.
Played varsity football.  Member Student
Council.  Boy's State alternate.  Earned
Kiwanis Citizenship Award senior year.
Sang with several boys' choral groups.

### Work Experience

Summer 1982       Carpenter's Assistant, Nordby Construction
Co., Billings, MT.  Helped in the
construction of several homes.  Learned
the basic skills of small building
carpentry.  Frequently worked alone after
receiving instructions from supervisor.

Summer 1981       General Laborer, Taylor Construction,
Bozeman, MT.  Assisted with all aspects of
residential and commercial building
construction including carpentry, concrete,
excavation, plumbing, wiring, and roofing.

Summer 1980       Flagman, Washington Construction,
Bozeman, MT.  Directed traffic around road
construction sites.

### Personal

Born:  April 11, 1965                    Health:  Excellent
Height:  6 feet                          Weight:  165 pounds
Interests:  Hunting, fishing, auto repair

### References

Available on request.

## RETAIL CLERK

BEVERLY UPDIKE

444 Elm Street
Castlewood, NM 45612                      Telephone: (404) 222-9801

### Occupational Objective

Part-time position as retail clerk

### Experience

1973 - 1975    Checker, K-Mart, Twin Butte, NM.  Operated cash
               register and occasionally assisted with
               inventory.  Served as substitute manager of
               women's clothing dept.

1969 - 1973    Checker, Gamble's Grocery Mart, Twin Butte, NM.
               Full-time checker.  Also helped stock shelves.

1968 - 1969    Checker, Ray's Quick Stop, Twin Butte, NM.

### Education

1964 - 1968    Sacred Heart High School, Twin Butte, NM.
               Took typing, shorthand, bookkeeping, and other
               general business courses.  Graduated 1968.

### General

Am reliable, experienced checker.  Left work in 1975 to
raise family.  Two children are now in school.

### Personal

Born:  November 9, 1950          Excellent health
Married; two children            Own home
Speak Spanish fluently

### References

Available on request.

## BANK TELLER

JANICE STREETER


Box 118
RR # 3
Rutledge, SD   54678
Telephone: (Home) 605-224-6743
          (Message) 605-224-9812


OBJECTIVE

Position as bank teller.

SUMMARY

Teller experience and good math abilities.

EXPERIENCE

Teller, First National Bank, Aberdeen, SD.  Performed all
standard duties of full-service bank teller.  1979 to 1982.

Teller, Farmer's State Bank, Kranzburg, SD.  Assisted with
preparation of loan contracts in addition to serving as
teller.  1974 to 1979.


EDUCATION

Watertown Senior High School, Watertown, SD.  Took advanced
math and bookkeeping courses.  Graduated 1973.


GENERAL

Have outgoing, friendly personality.  Relate well to
customers.  Am very good with figures.  Enjoy the atmosphere
of bank employment.

PERSONAL

Born:  June 1, 1955
Health:  Excellent
Married; two children (in school)
Interests:  sewing, poetry, gardening

REFERENCES

Available on request.

# ATTORNEY

RONALD K. KLEPPER

803C Donnavon Building
University of Nebraska
Lincoln, NE 22345
(302) 213-6701

## Resume Capsule

Third-year law student with military background.

## Objective

Position as attorney with United States Air Force.

## Education

1980 to Present     School of Law, University of Nebraska, Lincoln, NE. Will be awarded Juris Doctor Degree in spring of 1984. Member Phi Delta Phi legal fraternity. Won American Bar Association national award for academic excellence. Received scholarships from Omaha, NE, law firm last two years.

1976 to 1980       University of Nebraska, Lincoln, NE. B.A. Degree in secondary education. English major.

Participated 3 years in ROTC. Received following awards:
Distinguished Military Graduate (1980)
American Legion Citizenship Award
Distinguished Military Student (1980)
Army ROTC Outstanding Student Award
Also member ROTC Color Guard and University rifle team.

## Legal Experience

1982               Legal Intern, Nebraska Legal Services Association, Lincoln, NE. Handled

RONALD K. KLEPPER

landlord-tenant, debtor-creditor, custody, divorce, and other civil cases. Opened files, interviewed clients, arranged counseling, drafted documents, conducted direct and cross examinations, and represented clients at hearings. Earned an Award of Merit for OUTSTANDING ACHIEVEMENT from Nebraska Legal Services Association.

## Employment History

| | |
|---|---|
| Summer 1979 | Nebraska Power Co., Lincoln, NE. Served as assistant to the personnel director. |
| Summer 1978 | Omaha Tractor Parts, Inc., Omaha, NE. Worked on assembly line. |
| Summer 1977 | Osco Drug Store, Summerville, NE. Stocked shelves and did some checking. |

## Military Training

| | |
|---|---|
| 1976 to 1980 | * ROTC, University of Nebraska |
| 1980 | * ROTC Advanced Camp for Officer Training |
| 1980 to 1981 | * ROTC Special Survival Training |

## Affiliations

Association of United States Air Force
American Trial Lawyers' Association
Nebraska Student Lawyer Association

## Personal

Born:  February 3, 1958............Health:  Excellent
Height:  6 feet, one inch..........Weight:  170 pounds
Marital Status:  Single
Interests:  Canoeing, baseball, youth counseling

## References

Placement file available from Career Planning Office, University of Nebraska, Lincoln, NE 22346. Additional references available on request.

# DRAFTSMAN

Max Shaysted

1612 Mississippi Drive
St. Paul, MN 45098
(612) 222-3487

## Employment Record

<u>Draftsman</u>, Peak and Row, Inc., St. Paul, MN. Firm designs and builds equipment for scientific laboratories. Completed detail drafting on heat exchangers and pressure vessels. 1979 - 1982.

<u>Self-Employed Draftsman</u>, St. Paul, MN. Designed single-family and multi-family homes as well as commercial buildings. 1977 - 1979.

<u>Pipefitter/Maintenance Technician</u>, California Edison, Woodville, CA. Assembled and maintained piping on heat exchangers and pumps. Worked on hydraulic and pneumatic systems. 1972 - 1976.

<u>Pipefitter</u>, Lockwood Plumbing, Modesto, CA. Performed plumbing work on residential, commercial, and industrial facilities. 1968 - 1970.

<u>Production Welder</u>, Modesto Manufacturing, Inc., Modesto, CA. Firm makes auto body parts. 1965 - 1967.

## Education

<u>Modesto Community College</u>, Modesto, CA. Associate of Science Degree. Studied drafting and related technologies. 1963 - 1965.

## Military

U.S. Navy. Served as communications specialist on submarine. Honorable discharge. 1961 - 1963.

## References

Available on request.

## FORESTER

CECIL R. BILSTEIN

P.O. Box 7765
Yuma, AZ   45761
                                      Telephone:   446-223-7816

### Resume Capsule

Extensive experience in forestry, agriculture, range management, and wildlife restoration.

### Experience

6/78 to present
      and
9/63 to 7/73

RANGE CONSERVATIONIST/FORESTER, U.S. Forest Service.  Lead range analysis and planning teams throughout southwest region.  Revised range analysis handbook and developed assessment and recommendation program.  Write EIS.

Negotiate grazing fees.  Participate in wildlife and watershed studies.  Revise multiple use plans.  Supervised portions of RARE II.

Primary accomplishment has been consolidation of 21 grazing districts covering 9 counties and involving 11 different government entities.

Supervised 6-20 employees.

11/73 to 5/77

RANGE CONSERVATIONIST, U.S. State Dept., Linda Vista, Argentina.  Led team of range planners.  Assisted local conservationists in maximizing yield from native grasslands.  Instructed in techniques of managing forests, wildlife, water resources and agricultural crops and livestock.

### Education

1961 to present

Numerous classes and workshops on natural resource management and public program implementation.

## CECIL R. BILSTEIN


1956 to 1960        UNIVERSITY OF MONTANA, Missoula, MT.
                    B.S. Degree in resource management.


## Military

1950 to 1955        U.S. Army.  Honorable discharge


## Publications

"Range Husbandry in Argentina," Land Management Journal,
        Oct., 1958.
"Weed Control on Public Lands," American Forests, July,
        1980.
"Managing for Wildlife," Wildlife Journal, Sept., 1979.


## Personal

Born:  March 23, 1932
Health:  Excellent
Marital Status:  Married
Willing to travel
Location Preference:  Southwest U.S.
Interests:  Hunting, photography, spelunking


## References

Available on request.

## MEDICAL TECHNOLOGIST

RUBY DENTON

908 South Broadview
Hamilton, CO  40568
(313) 454-7791 (Home phone)
(313) 772-9832 (Message phone)

OCCUPATIONAL OBJECTIVE

Position as medical technologist.


EXPERIENCE

4/81 - Present      Medical Technologist, Mother of Mercy
                    Hospital, Denver, CO.  Perform wide
                    variety of laboratory work, including
                    phlebotomy, chemistry, urinalysis,
                    blood bank, and some special chemistry
                    lab work.  Also set up bacteriology
                    cultures.

2/77 - 1/81         Medical Technologist, Denver General
                    Hospital, Denver, CO.  Conducted full
                    range of lab work, including hematology,
                    serology, and special chemistry.

8/75 - 9/76         Intern, Denver General Hospital,
                    Denver, CO.  Became familiar with all
                    hospital laboratory functions.  Learned
                    procedures in bacteriology, chemistry,
                    virology, nuclear medicine, and pulmonary
                    function.


EDUCATION

1975 - 1976         Attended classes at University of Denver
                    while on internship.  Studied immunology.

RUBY DENTON

1970 - 1974          Kansas State University, Wichita, KS.
                     B.S. Degree in medical technology.
                     Studies emphasized medical aspects of
                     microbiology, mycology, virology, and
                     serology.


## CERTIFICATION

Registered Medical Technologist of American Society of
Clinical Pathology.


## PERSONAL

Born September 11, 1952
In excellent health
Married; two children


## REFERENCES

Available on request.

# ELECTRICIAN

THEODORE R. ROCKWELL

517 Kemp Ave.
Casper, WY  22387                    Telephone:  (616) 221-5648

## Resume Summary

Extensive background in industrial electrical work.

## Employment Objective

Position as electrical supervisor, preferably in the
electrified railroad field.

## Experience

1969 to Present     Owner, Casper Electrical Works, Casper,
                    WY.  Perform contract electrical work on
                    all types of buildings.  Employ 7
                    workers.

1951 to 1969        Electrification Foreman, Burlington
                    Northern Railroad, Cody, WY.  Supervised
                    up to 18 technicians in operation and
                    maintenance of 311 miles of electrified
                    rail.  Maintained and did troubleshooting
                    on substations using rotary converters.
                    Became proficient at engineering,
                    construction, and operation of catenary
                    facilities.  Received numerous awards
                    for crew safety.

## Education

1948 to 1950        Wyoming Institute of Technology.
                    Studied engineering and electronics.

1947                Carnell Institute, Boston, MA.  Took
                    basic electronics course of study.

THEODORE R. ROCKWELL

## Certification

Licensed journeyman electrical worker.

## Personal

Born: January 16, 1925                    Health: Excellent
Marital Status:  Married                  Residence: Owns home
Location Preference:  Willing to relocate and to travel
Interests:  Local politics, woodworking, reading

## References

Available upon request.

## CARPENTER

Roscoe Scally

1107 Roland Street
Harrington, MO   13476
222-454-6754

Job
Objective            Employment as journeyman carpenter.

Experience           11/80 - 3/82:  Randall Stinson Construction
                     Co., Jefferson City, MO.  Served as
                     construction supervisor.  Directed work of
                     other carpenters.  Framed, trimmed, and did
                     interior and exterior finish work.  Became
                     familiar with construction of residential
                     and commercial buildings.

                     6/78 - 4/80:  Self-employed contractor,
                     Osage, MO.  Performed all types of
                     subcontract work on single- and multi-family
                     dwellings, including framing, finishing,
                     ceramic tile installation, sheetrocking,
                     concrete work, roofing, and heating system
                     installation.  Employed one assistant.

                     9/76 - 4/78:  Valley Construction, Sioux
                     City, IA.  Employed as general carpenter.
                     Learned all phases of small building
                     construction.

                     7/74 - 5/76:  Sanders and Sons Contractors,
                     Sioux City, IA.  Apprentice carpenter.

Education             1970 - 1974:  Walt Whitman High School,
                     Sioux City, IA.  Took all available
                     woodworking and metal shop classes.
                     Graduated 1974.

Personal             Born:  August 2, 1955
                     Health:  Excellent
                     Marital Status:  Married; two children
                     Interests:  Hunting, fishing, bowling

General              Has own hand tools for general carpentry
                     jobs.  Can read blueprints.  Can do all
                     types of construction work except plumbing
                     and electrical.

References            Available on request.

# MANAGER (BUSINESS)

RESUME

Albert Davidson
666 Rimini Court
Hojack, MI    55346                Telephone:  (343) 222-4568


## OBJECTIVE

Position in business management.


## EMPLOYMENT RECORD

February 1978 -     Supervisor of Contracts, Tanner Trucking,
   June 1981        Springfield, MI.  Recruited owner/
                    operators for contract hauling of grain
                    and other commodities.  Traveled
                    extensively.  Prepared contracts.

December 1972 -     Owner/Manager, Hilltop Motel, Cranbrook,
   April 1975       British Columbia, Canada.  Performed all
                    management functions of 32-unit motel
                    operation, including hiring and firing,
                    bookkeeping, advertising, banking,
                    scheduling workers, and taxes.

October 1968 -      Owner, Montgomery Ward Catalog Store,
November 1972       Boise, ID.  Maintained showroom inventory
                    of appliances and tools and operated
                    complete catalog services.  Employed two
                    workers.

June 1965 -         Assistant Manager, Tower Pizza, Boise,
July 1968           ID.


## EDUCATION

September 1963 -    Idaho State University, Boise, ID.
   June 1965        Business administration major.

September 1957 -    Moscow Senior High School, Moscow, ID.
   May 1961         Graduated 1961.

Albert Davidson

## MILITARY

July 1961 -          U.S. Marine Corps.  Spent 18 months in
July 1963            Vietnam as U.S. Embassy guard.  Received
                     Meritorious Service Medal for defense of
                     embassy against terrorists.  Also
                     received Purple Heart.  Honorable
                     discharge.

## PERSONAL

Born July 4, 1945.......Health Excellent........Height 6'2"
Weight 175 lbs..........Married..........Willing to Relocate

## REFERENCES          Available on request.

# ACCOUNTANT

JASON T. WHITLOCK

1102 Madison Street
Crestview, IN  45674
(234) 656-1123

---

OBJECTIVE        Entry-level position with regional or
                 national accounting firm.  Advancement
                 potential a must.


EDUCATION:

1983             B.S. Degree in business administration,
                 University of Indiana, Calipso, IN.
                 Coursework emphasized accounting.  3.4 GPA
                 in major field.  Member Beta Alpha Psi
                 accounting fraternity.


EXPERIENCE:

6/77 to          Bookkeeper, Jacksons, Inc., Crestview, IN.
present          Firm sells jewelry and clothing.  Prepares
                 payroll, quarterly reports, and financial
                 statements.  Posts to general ledger.
                 Prepares operational budgets and computes
                 depreciation schedules.  Works part-time
                 while attending university.

5/78 to          Bookkeeper, Universal Athletics, Crestview,
present          IN.  Posts to general ledger, prepares
                 depreciation schedules, computes payroll,
                 and handles accounts payable.  Part-time
                 while attending university.

1/79 - 4/79      Tax Preparer, Wilson and Associates P.C.,
                 Crestview, IN.  Prepared individual and
                 corporate income taxes.  Part-time.

JASON T. WHITLOCK


3/73 - 7/74      Clerk/Bookkeeper, Allton Manufacturing
                 Company, Danville, OH.  Performed all
                 standard bookkeeping procedures under the
                 guidance of a CPA.


CERTIFICATION: Took CPA exam in May 1983.  Results
               available in August.


PERSONAL:        Born:  November 26, 1946
                 Single
                 Willing to Travel
                 Willing to Relocate


REFERENCES:      Available on request.

# TEACHER

Resume of SANDRA WILLIBEE

| | |
|---|---|
| Apt. #5, Kline Court | Home Phone: 605-887-2349 |
| Sioux Falls, SD 57684 | Message Phone: 605-726-6969 |

## POSITION DESIRED

High school English teacher.

## EMPLOYMENT HISTORY

Teacher, Clayton County Schools, Butte, NM, 1972 - 1976
>Taught English classes in grammar, literature, composition, and speech. Designed literature curriculum that is still in use. Created own teaching materials. Also served as advisor to staff of school newspaper and as director of junior class play.

Teacher, Kaiser High School, Oro, NM, 1969 - 1972
>Taught several sections of basic language skills to students with learning disabilities. Also coached school debate team.

Teacher, Dalton Junior High, Dalton, TX, 1965 - 1969
>Taught general English classes to grades 8 and 9.

## CERTIFICATION

Hold current South Dakota Secondary Teaching Certificate.

## EDUCATION

College of Sioux Falls, Sioux Falls, SD, 1981 - present
>Took 11 education credits on part-time basis to become recertified to teach. Classes were mostly concerned with methods of teaching English.

University of South Texas, Dalton, TX, 1961 - 1965
>B.S. Degree in education with English major. Speech minor. Recipient of creative writing award.

## SANDRA WILLIBEE

### GENERAL

Left teaching profession in 1976 to have baby.  Child is now
in school, and I am eager to return to a teaching career.

### PERSONAL

Born:  February 10, 1943
Health:  Excellent
Marital Status:  Married; one child
Location Preference:  Prefer Sioux Falls area

### REFERENCES

Teaching credentials available from Office of Career
Planning, University of South Texas, Dalton, TX 09805.
Additional references available upon request.

# LIFEGUARD

LISA McDANIEL

Room 221, Kelley Hall              Born:  April 3, 1960
Northern Arizona University        Health:  Excellent
Flagstaff, AZ  12765               Marital Status:  Single
Telephone:  909-371-3556           Height:  5 ft. 4 in.
                                   Weight:  130 lbs.


## Occupational Objective

Summer employment as swimming pool lifeguard

## Experience

Summer 1982    LIFEGUARD, Municipal Swimming Pool, Clay, AZ.
               Served as sole attendant for busy pool.  No
               reportable injuries occurred during the summer.
               On two occasions, pulled foundering child
               swimmers from pool.  Gave swimming and diving
               lessons.

Summer 1981    POOL ATTENDANT, Spartan Park, Jefferson, AZ.
               Sold tickets, cleaned pool, gave lessons,
               and occasionally assisted lifeguard.

## Qualifications

Have been certified in lifesaving and water safety
instruction by Red Cross.  Training included academic and
practical instruction in CPR and other advanced lifesaving
and water safety techniques.  Also have taken advanced swim
stroke classes.

## Education

1980 to        Northern Arizona University, Flagstaff, AZ.
present        Junior.  Physical Education major.  Have
               taken all available swim classes.

1975 to        Red Rocks Senior High School, Flagstaff, AZ.
 1980          Active in cheerleading, pep club, basketball,
               and track.

## References

Available upon request.

## NURSE

SAMANTHA T. WILCOX

1112 S. 8th Street
Pixtown, OH  34876                          Phone:  414-222-3421

OCCUPATIONAL OBJECTIVE

Position in nursing.

EXPERIENCE

1/77 - 8/82     Director of Staff Development, Mother of
                Mercy Hospital, Litchfield, CT.  Oriented new
                nurses to hospital.  Conducted in-service
                programs for all non-nursing departments,
                including physicians.  Planned and directed
                continuing education workshops.  Conducted
                CPR training and refresher courses.  Managed
                outreach programs to smaller hospitals in
                surrounding area.

                Oversaw all orientation activities related to
                complete staff transfer to new 180-bed
                hospital.  Instructed nurses and physicians
                in use of new communication and computer
                equipment.

6/75 - 2/76     Supervisor, ICU, CCU, and ER units, Community
                Hospital, Columbus, OH.  Scheduled and
                directed activities of eight nurses.
                Frequently had to be on hand at the beginning
                of each shift for instructional purposes.

8/74 - 5/75     Morning Supervisor, Orthopedic Unit, Clay
                Memorial Hospital, San Francisco, CA.
                Directed all activities of 11 nurses in
                110-bed orthopedic unit.

EDUCATION

1970 - 74       California State University, San Diego, CA.
                B.S. Degree in nursing.

## SAMANTHA T. WILCOX

1969          Graduated Clinton Senior High School,
              Clinton, CA.

### CERTIFICATION

10/74         Passed National Nursing Registry Exam.

### PERSONAL

Born:  September 12, 1948
Health:  Excellent
Marital Status:  Married; no children
Residence:  Owns home
Location Preference:  Pixtown area

### REFERENCES

Available upon request.

## SALESPERSON

Resume
of
James F. Doobie

Home Address:                          Business Address:
204 Siesta Lane                        669 Main Street
Little Rock, AR 34167                  Little Rock, AR 34168
(345) 666-8907                         (345) 459-9908

Experience

1978 - present     CALLAHAN REALTY, Little Rock, AR.  As
                   sales associate, deal with residential
                   and commercial properties.  Do some
                   door-to-door canvassing.  Completely
                   familiar with all aspects of real
                   estate business.

1975 - 1977        BENTON AUTO MALL, Little Rock, AR.  Sold
                   new and used cars.  Several times named
                   top salesman.

Education          UNIVERSITY OF LITTLE ROCK, Little Rock,
                   AR.  B.S. Degree 1975 in business.

Affiliations       University of Little Rock Alumni
                   Kiwanis Club
                   Lions Club
                   Arkansas Association of Realtors
                   Friends of the Library

Personal           Born August 8, 1956
                   Health excellent
                   Single
                   Willing to relocate and to travel

References         Available on request

# ADMINISTRATOR

Lucille K. Davis

134 Tulip Lane
Dunlop, AZ  34578                    Telephone:  (556) 334-7789

## Employment History

| | |
|---|---|
| 10/79 to present | <u>Director</u>, Arizona Radio Reading Service, Dunlop, AZ.  Service broadcasts 40 hours per week over closed circuit to blind and print-handicapped persons, dispersing local daily newspaper and magazine information.  As director, selects and prepares program information.  Recruits and trains volunteers. Promotes service throughout state.  Raises funds. |
| 1/79 to 9/79 | <u>Clerk</u>, Landlin's Distributing, Osage, TN. Firm distributes variety of textile products.  Handled mail and filing. Filled orders and rectified customer complaints. |
| 1973 to 1979 | Left work to raise a family.  Remained active as charity volunteer. |
| 1970 to 1973 | <u>Utility Worker</u>, Manville Plastics, Manville, OH.  Sorted and graded plastics for use in toys. |

## Education

| | |
|---|---|
| 1980 | Taylor Junior College, Dunlop, AZ. Took non-credit class in writing grants. |
| 1953 to 1957 | Jefferson High School, Jackson, MS. Involved in wide range of school and community activities. |

| | |
|---|---|
| <u>Volunteer Work</u> | Girl Scout Leader<br>Sunday School Teacher<br>United Way Campaign Worker<br>Red Cross<br>4-H |
| <u>Personal</u> | Health:  Excellent<br>Marital Status:  Married; 4 children<br>Interests:  Reading, handicrafts, music |
| <u>References</u> | Available on request. |

# GEOLOGIST

RESUME OF

Randall J. Dalton                              222 Pike's Peak Place
                                               Denver, CO 23234
                                               Telephone:  434-987-2134


## Occupational Objective

Position in field geology.


## Education

1978 - 83:              B.S. Degree in geology, University of
                        Colorado, Denver, CO.  Other academic
                        emphasis on chemistry and geography.
                        Financed education with summer and
                        night jobs.  2.8 GPA.  Member Alpha
                        Tau Beta Fraternity (president three
                        years).  Received $200 Chamber of
                        Commerce scholarship.


## Experience

Summer 1983:            Field Geologist, Rockville, UT.
                        Completed field geology course under
                        auspices of University of Colorado.
                        Conducted field mapping, using
                        topographic maps, air photos, and
                        Brunton compass.  Drafted maps at
                        night.  Intensive course required
                        12-14 hours of work per day.

Summer 1982:            Field Geologist, Murphy Geology
                        Consulting, Inc., Boulder, CO.
                        Assisted geologists in mapping land
                        for possible use as MX Missile base.
                        Learned to operate all standard field
                        geologist's tools.

Randall J. Dalton


Summers 1980 & 81:    <u>Crew Member</u>, Allied American, Inc.,
                      Canesville, CO.  Firm does geology
                      consulting.  Worked out of remote camp
                      in mapping oil exploration sites.
                      Performed reconnaissance work and
                      conducted field mapping.

1978 to present:      <u>Bartender</u>, Town House Inn, Denver, CO.
                      Mixed drinks, closed up, and banked
                      receipts for exclusive supper club.
                      Worked 25-30 hours per week at night
                      during school year.


## General

Have outgoing personality.  Enjoy hard work and long hours.
Prefer to work out-of-doors.  Dependable.


## Personal

Born:  April 16, 1958
Health:  Excellent
Interests:  Bicycling, rock music, swimming
Will relocate anywhere in U.S.


## References

Available on request

## JOURNALIST

JOSEPH R. BELINI

1209 Kline Drive
Cherokee, OK   23980                    Telephone:   212-342-7656

### Resume Summary

Experienced editor, reporter, and columnist.

### Experience

11/73 to        GENERAL ASSIGNMENT REPORTER, FEATURE WRITER,
present:        AND COLUMNIST, Oklahoman, Dunkirk, OK.
                Newspaper is morning daily with 12,000
                circulation.  Began as police and court
                reporter.  Served 1-½ years as city editor,
                supervising complete staff of reporters and
                photographers.  Also served as sports and
                business editor for brief periods.
                Presently covers breaking news, writes feature
                articles, and produces weekly outdoor column.
                Thoroughly familiar with standard newspaper
                computer systems.

7/70 to         ASSOCIATE PROFESSOR OF JOURNALISM, University
 6/73:          of Tulsa, Tulsa, OK.  Taught all basic
                reporting and editing classes as well as
                photography workshops and seminars on
                journalism ethics.  Served as advisor to
                journalism graduate students.

2/69 to         ASSISTANT PROFESSOR OF JOURNALISM, Department
 6/70:          of Journalism, Central State College, San
                Antonio, TX.  Taught beginning and advanced
                reporting, journalism for high school teachers,
                photo-journalism, grammar for journalists, and
                public relations.  Advised staff of daily
                student newspaper.

1/66 to         GENERAL ASSIGNMENT REPORTER AND PHOTOGRAPHER,
 8/67:          Billings Gazette, Billings, MT.  Newspaper is
                an afternoon daily with circulation of 65,000.
                Covered variety of news assignments.  Also
                wrote features and reported on sports.
                Frequently functioned as city editor in that
                person's absence.

## JOSEPH R. BELINI

### Education

9/67 to    Central State College, San Antonio, TX.
  1/69:    Graduate assistant in department of journalism.
           Awarded $2,000 scholarship from American Legion
           Foundation.  Earned 3.4 GPA.  Received Master's
           Degree in journalism.  Thesis (on press coverage
           of Gulf of Tonkin incident) later published in
           three major journalism journals.

1965:      University of South Dakota, Vermillion, SD.
           B.S. Degree in journalism.  English and biology
           minors.  Member Sigma Tau Delta and Kappa Tau
           Alpha, English and journalism honorary
           fraternities.  Worked way through school as cub
           reporter on local paper.

### Military

8/59 to    U.S. Army.  Served as tank mechanic on several
  8/61:    posts in Germany.  Honorable discharge.

### Special Publications

* Trout Fishing in the South, 250-page, hardcover guide to
  fishing the waters of nine southern states.
* Backwoods Survival Guide, 400-page, paperback.  Now in
  fifth printing.
* Numerous articles for hunting, fishing, backpacking, skiing,
  and canoeing magazines.  Complete list available on request.

### Personal

Born:  January 11, 1940              Health:  Excellent
Height:  5 feet, 11 inches           Weight:  295 pounds
Marital Status:  Single
Interests:  Hunting, photography, golf, reading
Willing to relocate
Willing to travel

### References

References and complete publication portfolio available
upon request.

# ACCOUNTANT

JEFFREY ALAN TORGERSON

| | |
|---|---|
| 1160 Mendell Lane | Born: Sept. 3, 1960 |
| Nashville, TN | Willing to Relocate |
| Phone:  454-236-7783 | Marital Status:  Single |

Education:      Tennessee College of Business, Ragtown, TN.
                B.S. Degree in business administration.
                Accounting major.  Studied taxes, auditing,
                cost accounting, and management.  1978-1982.

                Grand High School, Country Square West,
                Nashville, TN.  Took all available accounting
                and bookkeeping classes.  1974-1978.

Experience:     Montgomery Ward and Co., Nashville, TN.
                Began in catalog dept. and later promoted to
                bookkeeper.  Operated receiving dept.,
                reconciled bank statements, and maintained
                accounts payable.  Also handled purchase
                orders, invoices, and requisitions.
                Part-time during school and full-time
                summers.  1974-1982.

General:        Has taken CPA exam and will have results in
                August.  Seeks entry-level employment that
                could lead to career position.  Handles
                responsibility well and enjoys being a part
                of office staff.

References:     Available on request.

# LOBBYIST

Beverly Bradley
201 Mission Drive
Sacramento, CA 09891
213-567-4434

-----------------------------------------------------------

## Professional Objective

Position as legislative lobbyist.

## Education

B.S. Degree, Sacramento State College, Sacramento, CA.
Political Science major.  Studies emphasized legislative
process and public administration.  Participated in
internship program at state legislature.  Graduated 1983.

## Experience

Lobbyist Intern, California State Legislature,
Sacramento, CA.  Worked with lobbyists for fishing and
agriculture industries.  Read and studied bills.  Attended
meetings and strategy sessions.  Became thoroughly familiar
with legislative process, political timing, Sacramento
personalities, and the effective use of legislation.  1981.

## Personal

Born January 2, 1958
Single
Willing to Relocate
Willing to Travel

## References

On file at Placement Office, Sacramento State College,
Sacramento, CA 09890.

## CUSTODIAN

GRACE WHITNEY

1911 Seymour Street
Bakersfield, NV 90734                    Telephone:   909-232-7691

Occupational Objective:    Employment as custodian.

Qualifications:            Homemaker and mother for 24 years.
                           Have become proficient at painting,
                           cleaning, carpet care, lawn care, basic
                           plumbing and electrical repairs, and
                           troubleshooting appliance repair.  Have
                           assisted in basement refinishing,
                           garage construction, and some home
                           concrete work.

                           Worked full-time as nurse's aid at
                           large hospital.  Among other duties,
                           performed maintenance tasks such as
                           floor care.

                           Have held various jobs as supermarket
                           checker, secretary, and retail clerk.

                           Have operated part-time businesses out
                           of home.

Education:                 Danville, Senior High School,
                           Danville, CT.  Graduated.

General:                   Looking for full-time, long-term
                           custodial employment.  Learn quickly
                           and work hard.  Follow instructions
                           well and need no supervision.

Personal:                  Health is excellent.  Married with
                           three adult children.  Own home.

References:                Available on request.

## MANAGER (BUSINESS)

GREGORY DONALDSON

501 Sunnydale Drive
Mansfield, OH  44501                    Telephone:  (921) 345-6543


### Professional Objective

Business management position requiring organization, accuracy,
and judgment skills.  Am eager to fully utilize business
education and experience.

### Areas of Accomplishment

Management       Served as assistant department manager for
Abilities:       large, diversified sporting goods firm.
                 Participated in all aspects of department
                 operation.  Created several successful
                 promotions that helped increase sales 25
                 percent over two years.  Supervised up to
                 five clerks.  Became thoroughly familiar
                 with retail operation.

Sales            Sold all types of men's clothing.
Abilities:       Counseled customers and became adept at
                 closing sales quickly.  Was consistently
                 top salesman in the store.  Earned frequent
                 bonuses for sales accomplishments.

Other            Worked part-time and summers as stock boy,
Experience:      carpenter's helper, delivery driver, and
                 custodian.

### Education

B.S. Degree in Business Administration with concentrations
in accounting and management.  University of Ohio, York, OH.
Graduated 1979.

### Employers

    Lambert's Dept. Store, York, OH.  1979-1982.
    Mr. Carl's, York, OH.  1971-1975.

### Personal                          ### References

Born:  January 4, 1949              Available on request
Single
Health:  Excellent
Willing to relocate

## LABORER

Resume of NICK BANNER

P.O. Box 447
Castlewood, AR                    Message Phone:  212-667-8793

JOB OBJECTIVE      Employment as general laborer.

AREAS OF EXPERIENCE

   Construction Trades:  Have worked as assistant to
   carpenters, plumbers, dry-wallers, roofers, and
   electricians.  Familiar with techniques and tools of
   these trades.

   Agricultural:  Have cared for cattle, sheep, and
   horses on small-medium farms and ranches.  Can operate
   tractors, balers, forklifts, milking machines, and
   other agricultural equipment.  General knowledge of
   animal nutrition and grain crop techniques.

   Mechanical:  Can do basic automotive repair, including
   tune-ups, tire work, muffler and shock installation,
   and some bodywork.  Familiar with most general shop
   tools.

EDUCATION

   Whitman High School, Pierre, SD.  Graduated 1958.

PERSONAL

   Health:  Good                    Height:  6 feet
   Marital Status:  Single          Weight:  165 pounds

REFERENCES

   Available on request.

# POLICE OFFICER

STEPHEN McFARLAND


Box 118
Danner Creek Road
Mount Blackburn, CT 23451
Telephone: (414) 778-9812


Professional Goal:        Management position on rural or
                          small-town police force.


## Qualifications

LAW ENFORCEMENT/INVESTIGATION: Skilled in police
work related to traffic control, fingerprinting, crowd
control, investigative photography, and explosives.
Have conducted background investigations. Performed
counterintelligence activities for U.S. Army. Have
coordinated police coverage of marches and
demonstrations. Familiar with small-force police
procedures.

Management: Have supervised up to 85 subordinates.
Familiar with all aspects of office and personnel
management. Have prepared, revised, and corrected
investigative reports. Can prepare budgets and
allocate funds. Can train personnel in small arms
use, photography, self-defense, and other police
procedures.


## Military

U.S. Army: Served in Korea, Germany, and Vietnam.
Duty assignments always entailed police and/or
intelligence operations. Achieved rank of major.
Awarded Purple Heart and three Medals of Special
Citation.


## Education

University of New Jersey, Trenton, NJ. B.S. Degree
in education. Biology and psychology majors.

STEPHEN McFARLAND

## General

Grew up in rural Connecticut.  Familiar with
lifestyles, mores, and attitudes of people.

## Personal

Health:  Excellent
Height:  Five feet, eleven inches
Weight:  180 pounds
Location Preference:  Rural Connecticut
Willing to relocate

## References

Available on request.

# PHARMACIST

---

JOANN BARRETT


1919 East Spruce
Summerville, IN  46235          Telephone (202) 344-6611


## Professional Objective

Position as staff pharmacist in medium-sized hospital.


## Experience

Presently employed in hospital pharmacy.  Fill prescriptions
    for inpatients and outpatients.  Check drug interaction
    and question dosage.  Use demand unit dose system.
    Supervise student interns from university.

Have performed numerous drugstore duties, including serving
    as sole pharmacist and as store manager.  Supervised up
    to four employees, ordered stock, conducted inventory,
    set prices, and did banking.

Have served as pharmacist in government institutions.
    Worked with retarded, alcoholic, and terminally ill.


## Employers

Summerville Memorial Hospital, Summerville, IN
Indiana State Hospital for the Mentally Retarded, Cory, IN
Timmerman's Pharmacy, Indianapolis, IN
David's Discount Pharmacy, Indianapolis, IN
U.S. Veteran's Hospital, Danube, IN
Paulson Drug Store, Danube, IN


## Education

University of Chicago, Chicago, IL.  B.S. Degree in
pharmacy.  3.0 GPA.

JOANN BARRETT

## Licenses and Certifications

Registered Pharmacist, State of Indiana
Registered Pharmacist, State of Illinois
Hospital Pharmacist Certification, State of Indiana

## Affiliations

American Pharmaceutical Association
Indiana Pharmaceutical Association
Indiana Society of Hospital Pharmacists
National Association of Retail Pharmacists

## Personal

Health:  Excellent
Marital Status:  Single
Willing to relocate
Interests:  Volunteer work, church groups, bird watching

## References

Available upon request.

# OPTICIAN

GLORIA DAVENPORT

Apt. 115
Westview Village
Denver, CO  56023                    Telephone:  (234) 345-6754

## Occupational Objective

Employment as a dispensing optician in locally owned
optical shop.  Eventually would like to manage optical shop.

## Qualifications

Optician        Have 12 years experience as optician.
                Measure and dispense all types of lenses
                and frames.  Can cut, edge, and tint
                lenses.  Adept at adjustment and minor frame
                repair.  Experience in physicians' offices
                and in retail shops.

Management      Have performed all types of bookkeeping
                in optical shop setting.  Can maintain
                inventory and supply control.  Familiar
                with advertising techniques and all other
                aspects of office operation.  Have managed
                shops for short periods and trained new
                employees.

## Education

WESTERN COLORADO VOCATIONAL CENTER, Denver, CO.  Completed
courses in business management and optician training.

HAWTHORN SENIOR HIGH SCHOOL, Pike, CO.  Graduated.

Personal                              References

Excellent health                      Available on request.
Prefer Denver area
Married
Own home

## VARIED BACKGROUND—BUSINESS/INSURANCE/CONSTRUCTION

Resume of:


ROBERT K. KAUFMAN                      Born: June 6, 1940
903 Sparwood Street                    Health: Excellent
Boston, MA  13781                      Married; two children
Phone:  412-443-5601                   Will relocate


Areas of Expertise

    Tax Preparation:  Capable of preparing all forms of
        taxes for individuals and small businesses.
        Skilled at searching for legitimate deductions.
        Advises client on recordkeeping and tax
        preparation for coming year.  Familiar with
        all recent tax law changes.

    Insurance:  Sold complete range of life, health,
        and casualty insurance.  Wrote specialty
        policies.  Trained new salesmen.

    Construction:  Skilled at most phases of home
        construction, including carpentry, electrical,
        roofing, and concrete work.  Operates all
        standard construction equipment.


Education

    Boston State College.  Three years as math
    major.  3.9 GPA.


Military

    U.S. Air Force.  Served in Vietnam as language
    instructor.  Honorable discharge.


References

    Available on request.

## TIMBER BROKER

---

Resume of

PETER F. PORTER

#17 Mink Ranch Road
Casper, WY  34567

### Professional Objective

Position as timber broker.

### Experience

TIMBER BROKER
Formed and serves as president of Wind River Timber
Company, Casper, WY.  Firm acts as timber broker for
regional developers, contractors, and wholesalers.
Personally selects sale lots.  Contracts with buyers
and arranges transportation.  Employs five workers.
Has produced average annual volume increase of 18
percent.  Has become thoroughly familiar with American
and international timber market and supply.  1974 to
present.

CONSTRUCTION CONTRACTOR
Formed Casper Construction Co., Casper, WY.  Firm
builds residential and small commercial buildings.
Employed 12 workers at peak.  Solicited contracts,
kept books, advertised, and performed all other small
business managerial functions.  Began in 1967.  Sold
business in 1974.

### Education

Casper County Vocational School, Casper, WY.  Completed
two-year construction program.  1964 to 1966.

Rocky Mountain High School, Landers, WY.  Graduated 1963.

### Personal                                        ### References

Born:  July 16, 1945                   Available on request
Health:  Good
Marital Status:  Single
Willing to do extensive travel
Willing to relocate

## MANAGER/SALESPERSON

DONNA KINGSLEY

42 Wentworth Avenue                    Home Phone: 406-345-6573
Cedar Falls, MI   22396              Message Phone: 406-345-2132

### Resume Summary

Skilled in management, sales, and office work.  Areas of
expertise include furniture, mobile homes, cosmetics,
food, and hardware.  Has had great deal of contact with
buying public.

### Qualifications

Management:     Served in numerous managerial capacities
                in furniture, cosmetics, and restaurant
                businesses.  Supervised employees,
                ordered and received merchandise,
                stocked, and conducted inventory.
                Banked receipts, prepared budgets, and
                calculated prices.  Assisted in
                selecting lines of merchandise.
                Prepared work schedules and store
                displays.  Wrote newspaper ads and
                created TV and radio commercials.

Sales:          Sold all types of home furnishings.
                Counseled customers and made in-home
                consultations.  Traveled extensive
                route as sales representative of major
                cosmetics firm.  Gave lectures and
                demonstrations.  Assisted customers with
                displays.  Also has sold mobile homes.
                Familiar with all types of sales
                contracts.

Clerical:       Has handled accounts payable and
                receivable.  Types and operates 10-key
                adder, validating machine, and Xerox.
                Also experienced at filing,
                correspondence, posting, payroll,
                costing, and bank reconciliations.

DONNA KINGSLEY

## Employers

The Furniture Emporium, Cedar Falls, MI.  1976 to present.
    True Value Hardware, Cedar Falls, MI. 1970 to 1972.
    Bonne Bell Cosmetics, Lakewood, OH.  1969 to 1970.
Macy's Department Store, San Francisco, CA.  1967 to 1969.
    Dickerman's Drug, Cedar Falls, MI.  1965 to 1966.
        Rexall Drug, Cedar Falls, MI.  1963 to 1965.

## Education

Jefferson County High School, Cedar Falls, MI.  Graduated
1964.  General course of study with emphasis on art and
clerical skills.

## General

Is resourceful, talented salesperson whose strong point is
customer contact.  Interested in working into management
position.  Has outgoing personality.

## Personal

Health:  Excellent
Born:  September 2, 1946
Travel:  Willing to do some
Marital Status:  Married; one child
Residence:  Owns home; husband employed in Cedar Falls
Interests:  Writing poetry, painting, fishing, sewing

## References

Available on request.

# WAITRESS

ANDREA MACK

Apt. F
555 Kingston Ave.
Houston, TX  45680                   Telephone:  323-777-8921


JOB OBJECTIVE:    Employment as restaurant waitress.


WORK HISTORY:    Red Lion Lodge, San Antonio, TX.  Served
                 as waitress shift supervisor and as
                 waitress.

                 Billy's Cafe, San Antonio, TX.  Waitress.

                 Four D's Restaurant, San Antonio, TX.
                 Waitress.

                 The Black Steer, Austin, TX.  Waitress.


SKILLS:          * Can schedule shifts and supervise workers.
                 * Able to personally handle many tables.
                 * Can work under pressure.
                 * Good math skills.
                 * Familiar with all standard restaurant
                   practices.
                 * Am neat, punctual, and have pleasant
                   personality.


EDUCATION:       Sam Houston High School, El Paso, TX.
                 Graduated.


PERSONAL:        In excellent health
                 Married; children in school


REFERENCES:      Available on request.

## SECRETARY

Resume
of
Doris Appelhoff

119 Skiskin Road                          Born:  March 1, 1949
Badger, Vermont  13561                    Married; no children
Phone:  909-652-9982                      Will relocate

Objective:  Employment as personal secretary.

Capabilities:

    * Type 72 words per minute
    * Operate word processors
    * Take dictation effectively
    * Excellent telephone manner
    * Good organizational skills
    * High standards of neatness and accuracy
    * Knowledge of small business practices

Formal Training:

NORTH VERMONT VOCATIONAL SCHOOL, Hanover, VT.  Attended
secretarial program for one year.

ROSEHILL HIGH SCHOOL, Rosehill, VT.  Graduated.  Took many
bookkeeping, accounting, and office practice classes.

Employers:

        Davidson and Barker, Attorneys, Hanover, VT.
            Carter's Department Store, Preston, VT.
        Cecil Rhoades Secretarial Services, Boston, MA.
            Larry Larson Insurance Co., Badger, VT.

References

Available on request.

## GUIDE

RAY GREENFIELD

P.O. Box 2357
Sheridan, WY  45371                    Telephone:  616-445-8780


JOB OBJECTIVE:

Employment as guide, wrangler, or cook with backcountry
outfitter.

AREAS OF EXPERIENCE:

Guiding:  Have worked as wilderness hunting and fishing
     guide in variety of backcountry areas.  Familiar with
     techniques for hunting elk, deer, moose, and bear.
     Work well with clients who have little hunting
     experience.  Clients have always achieved high hunting
     success ratio.

Wrangling:  Thoroughly familiar with and comfortable
     around horses.  Have been solely responsible for pack
     strings of up to 20 head.  Can teach non-horsemen how
     to ride in a short time.

Cooking:  Have served as cook in backcountry camps.
     Know how to prepare good meals for large group.  Used
     to working under difficult conditions with bare
     minimum of equipment.

EDUCATION:

Sheridan Central High School, Sheridan, WY.  Graduated
     1977.  Participated in all sports.

GENERAL:

Am outgoing person who does not mind long hours.  Greatly
enjoy the out-of-doors and the atmosphere of a backcountry
camp.  Am conscientious employee.

PERSONAL:

Born -- 1959                        Height -- 5'11"
Health -- Excellent                 Weight -- 175 lbs.

REFERENCES:

Available on request.

## ACCOUNTANT/MANAGER

EILEEN F. SPOON

201 Centerville Terrace
Terrytown, UT 45672
904-674-9823

Employment Objective:        Managerial position with an
                             accounting firm.

Qualifications:

ACCOUNTING/BOOKKEEPING:  Full charge bookkeeper.  Can
    prepare quarterly reports and payrolls, ready accounts
    for audits, handle accounts receivable and payable, and
    post charges and receipts.  Can keep complete books for
    proprietors, partnerships, and corporations.  Also do
    light auditing.

TAX PREPARATION:  Prepare heavy income tax returns using
    Unitax, Computax, and Accutax systems.  Interview
    clients and ready material for computer.

OFFICE MANAGEMENT:  Supervise complete accounting systems.
    Reconcile cash drawers.  Can be responsible for dozens
    of sets of books at once.  Can supervise other
    employees.

OFFICE SKILLS:  Handle telephone, mail, typing, and other
    secretarial duties.  Operate electric and manual
    typewriters, 10-key, NCR bookkeeping machine, and Xerox
    copier.  Also some work on word processor.

Employers:

Garlington, Stoffer, and French, CPA, Salt Lake City, UT.
    1979 to present.
Martin Matthews, CPA, Salt Lake City, UT.  1976 to 1979.
Rosenbloom and Associates, PC, Ogden UT.  1971 to 1974.
Carry and Matovitch, CPA, Salt Lake City, UT.  1969 to 1971.

EILEEN F. SPOON

Education:

* Fairview County Vocational School, Salt Lake City, UT.
Courses in word processing, business law, and computers.
1980 to 1981.

* Ogden Community College, Ogden, UT.  Secretarial skills
refresher course.  1973.

* North Dakota State Teachers College, Mandan, ND.
Majored in elementary education.  1955 to 1957.


Personal:

Born:                              August 29, 1937
Marital Status:                    Married; 3 adult children
Residence:                         Own home
Location Preference:               Salt Lake City area
Interests:                         Travel, beadwork, reading


References:  Available on request.

# PHOTOGRAPHER

RAYMOND ALAN DICKERMAN

22 Crane Circle --- Medford, OR 99345 --- 808-667-4569

## Professional Goal

Position as studio, newspaper, or magazine photographer.

## Skills

Studio Photography:  Several years experience in shooting
all types studio photography:  graduation, passport,
anniversary, Christmas card, baby, and pet.  Familiar with
studio lighting techniques.  Works well with customers.

Photojournalism:  Has sold photographs to newspapers on
freelance basis.  Acquainted with newspaper requirements
for timely photos delivered by deadline.  Knowledgeable in
35mm and larger formats.  Able to develop and print all
types black and white film.

Magazine Photography:  Has sold hundreds of photos to
national magazines on freelance basis:  scenics, people,
industrial, wildlife, mood photos, and others.  Consistently
has filled specific needs of magazines such as Sierra,
National Wildlife, Newsweek, Parents, Science Digest,
and others.

Darkroom Work:  Thoroughly familiar with all modern
darkroom techniques with 35mm color and black and white
photography.

## Portfolio

A complete portfolio of published photographs and studio
work is available upon request.

RAYMOND ALAN DICKERMAN

## Education

University of Iowa, Ames, IA.  Journalism major.
Attended three years.  Took all photography courses
offered.

## Military

U.S. Army.  Three-year enlisted tour.  Served in Vietnam.
Honorable discharge.

## Personal

Born:  Nov. 10, 1950.....................Health: Excellent
Height:  Six feet, one inch...............Weight: 180 lbs.
Willing to relocate......................Willing to travel
Marital Status:  Single............Speaks Spanish fluently

## References

Available on request.

## RETAIL SALESPERSON

Steven Goodfellow

801 Harrison Ave.
Little Rock, AR 33432
(786) 254-9826

Occupational Objective

Position in retail sales or management.

Employment History

Manager, North Side Pharmacy, Little Rock, AR. 1976 to
present. Scheduled and directed activities of two
pharmacists and three clerks. Assisted pharmacists in
filling prescriptions. Attended to all details of small
business operation, including bookkeeping, banking,
advertising, pricing, and payroll.

Manager, Sporting Goods Dept., Dunkelberg's Department
Store, Raleigh, NC. 1973 to 1976. Supervised four
employees. Had complete autonomy in ordering and display
of merchandise, advertising, and other aspects of
department operation.

Salesman, Tremper's Fine Fashions, Atlanta, GA. 1970 to
1973. Firm is largest men's clothing retailer in Atlanta.
Sold all types of apparel. Won several awards for
salesmanship. Occasionally oversaw all store activities
in manager's absence.

Salesman, KC Foods, Inc., Orlando, FL. 1968 to 1970.
Firm specializes in home delivery of frozen foods. Made
cold contacts in homes. Was consistently among top 10
salesmen in staff of 25.

Education

University of South Florida, Orlando, FL, 1967 to 1968.
Took business and psychology classes.

<u>Steven Goodfellow</u>


<u>Central High School</u>, Orlando, FL, 1958 to 1962.
Graduated.



## <u>Military</u>

<u>U.S. Air Force</u>, 1963 to 1967.  Served in Germany as
radio communications technician.  Honorable discharge.



## <u>Personal</u>

Born:  August 14, 1944                    Health: Excellent
Marital Status:  Married                  Willing to Relocate


## <u>References</u>

Available upon request.

# MANAGER (GOVERNMENT)

HOWARD KLEINSCHMIDT

908 Elm Avenue
Bismarck, ND  56743                    Telephone:  (806) 345-4356

## Professional Objective

Managerial position, preferably with U.S. Government or
heavy industry.

## Resume Capsule

Possess a number of managerial and communication skills as
well as technical expertise.

## Qualifications

Managerial:  Owned own plumbing business.  Employed and
supervised crew doing all manner of plumbing in single-family
and multi-tenant dwellings.  Negotiated contracts, computed
payroll, and kept books.  Also have served as park ranger,
organizing and supervising recreational activities.  Managed
park visitor center.  Managed retail clothing store and
conducted all activities pursuant to retail operation:
advertising, banking, personnel relations, inventory,
ordering, etc.

Communications:  As park ranger, created and conducted
interpretive presentations.  Gave guided tours.  Designed
programmed electronic instruction.  Wrote informational
literature.  Authored conservation easement handbook,
engineering reports, annotated bibliography on recreational
topics, and environmental law briefs.  Made numerous formal
presentations and taught classes.

Technical:  Have served as engineer's aid and have been
involved with recreational site construction.  Read
blueprints.  Skilled at plumbing and related construction
activities.  Familiar with railroad rules, safety, and
maintenance guidelines.  Have done some computer programming.

HOWARD KLEINSCHMIDT

## Employers

Kansas-Pacific Central Railroad, Topeka, KS
National Park Service, Theodore Roosevelt National Park, ND
North Dakota Park Service, Bismarck, ND
Donaldson's Fine Fashions, Topeka, KS
U.S. Department of Agriculture

## Education

University of Kansas, Wentworth, KS.  B.A. Degree in
resource conservation.  Minors in sociology and
interpersonal communications.

## Personal

Born:  May 10, 1951                Health:  Excellent
Height:  6 feet, 2 inches       Weight:  200 pounds
Marital Status:  Single
Leisure Activities:  Photography, motorcycles, woodworking

## References

Available through Placement Division, University of Kansas,
Wentworth, KS.

# TEACHER

Todd Bannack


11 Highway Way
Goodwin, WA   23214
982-445-8723


## Employment Objective

Position as music or English teacher, possibly in
combination with assistant principalship.


## Teaching Experience

<u>Taught</u> high school orchestra, band, composition, drama,
and debate.  Directed local adult theaters and school
productions such as "South Pacific" and "Hello Dolly."
Produced Christmas concerts.  Sponsored school music club
and advised school newspaper staff.  Eleven years.  Seattle
Public Schools, Seattle, WA.

<u>Taught</u> elementary and secondary band and chorus.  Served
as sole classroom music instructor for school of 300
students.  Three years.  Corvallis, OR.

<u>Taught</u> special creative writing workshops for gifted
children, ages 10 through 18.  Devised challenging writing
projects for pilot program that has since been copied
elsewhere.  One year.  Sand Point, ID.


## Supervisory Experience

Has functioned as temporary principal in elementary and
secondary schools.  Summer work has included supervision
of 4- to 10-man crews in construction and general labor
trades.  As U.S. Air Force officer, oversaw communications
facilities for entire base, including about 80 technicians.
Familiar with work schedules, performance reports, and all
other aspects of personnel supervision.

Todd Bannack

## Education

Master of Education Degree, University of Wyoming, Cody, WY.
Degree is in public school administration.  Earned 3.6 GPA.

B.S. Degree in Education, Fillmore State College, Devil's
Lake, WA.  Majors in music and English.  Minor in math.
Active in intramurals, drama, and band.

## Certification

Holds Washington and Oregon secondary teaching certificates
with endorsements in music, English, and math.

## Affiliations

Washington Teachers Association
National Education Association
Phi Delta Chi
American Legion
Boy Scouts of America (troop leader)

## Military

U.S. Air Force.  Achieved rank of captain during four-year
tour.  Served as communications squadron commander.
Honorable discharge.

## Personal

Born January 17, 1934
In excellent health
Married, three children
Willing to relocate
Interests include music composition, hunting, fishing

## References

Available on request.

## ADVERTISING AGENT

<u>RESUME</u>                     <u>RESUME</u>                     <u>RESUME</u>

Ellen Sichrist.......407 Hill Street.......Buffalo, NY 09871
Home Phone 202-665-7812...........Message Phone 202-546-2238

### O B J E C T I V E

To help your advertising agency do a better job of promoting
your clients.

HERE'S WHAT I CAN DO FOR YOU:

    *** Write top-notch advertising copy for print ads
    *** Write and direct radio and TV spots
    *** Create slogans and themes for any ad campaign
    *** Work with clients to determine their exact needs
    *** Shoot production-quality photographs
    *** Guide paste-up workers in achieving image goals
    *** Conceive total, beginning-to-end promotions
    *** Work well as part of a team

HERE'S WHAT I'VE DONE FOR OTHERS:

    *** Managed all phases of SUCCESSFUL congressional
        ad programs
    *** Guided makers of new products in profitable ad
        campaigns
    *** Written promotional articles that have been
        published in dozens of magazines and newspapers
    *** Created, directed, and appeared in TV and radio
        ads
    *** Assisted clients in restructuring advertising
        after negative publicity
    *** Done extensive layout and paste-up of print ads

### E D U C A T I O N

UNIVERSITY OF MISSOURI.  B.A. Degree in journalism.  1976.

### G E N E R A L

Am energetic, outgoing, friendly, confident, and competent.
Know the advertising business well.  Comfortable working
with large and small client firms.  Don't mind long hours.
Work well without supervision.

### R E F E R E N C E S   A N D   P O R T F O L I O

Available upon your request

## DISK JOCKEY

LANCE BUCKLEW **** 119 Oak St., Butte, MT **** 406-223-7865


RADIO STATION MANAGERS:     LOOKING FOR SOMEONE TO LIVEN UP
                            THOSE LATE NIGHT BROADCAST HOURS?

                            NEED SOMEONE TO PULL LISTENERS AWAY
                            FROM YOUR COMPETITION?

                            WANT A DYNAMIC ON-AIR PERSONALITY
                            WHO CAN ATTRACT ADVERTISERS?


BUCKLEW IS THE NAME AND RADIO IS MY GAME ... and I play it
well!  I can:

                    ...Create and conduct talk shows...

                  ...Play music with the best of them...

                    ...Report hard news and sports...

                          ...Do remotes...

                    ...Conduct special promotions...

                     ...Write advertising copy...

                      ...Sell advertising...

                      ...Plan show formats...

              ...Do interviews for public service features...

                    ...Perform in advertising spots...


            I HAVE A JOURNALISM DEGREE AND YEARS OF EXPERIENCE
            I AM RELIABLE, FRIENDLY, OUTGOING, AND AGGRESSIVE
            I KNOW MOST OF THE TRICKS OF THE BROADCAST TRADE
                    I AM TOO GOOD TO PASS UP


.......So, give me a call and let me tell you exactly what
I can do for you.  Better not wait.  The competition may get
to me first!!!!!!!!!!!!!!!!!!!!!!!!!!!!!!!!!!!!!!!!!!!!!!!!!!!

# Chapter 7

# THE INTERVIEW

Voilà! Your diligent job search is paying off. Your resumes and cover letters have gone out, and a firm (or two or three) has asked you to come in for an interview. Your resume's job is now largely complete, and you must depend on a different set of skills to take you successfully through the interview process.

Your prospective employer probably has narrowed the field of candidates to two or three, so your chances of getting the job are quite good. That employer sees the interviews as a way to make the final determination about which of you will be offered the job. For him/her, the difference between hiring the best candidate and the second best may be thousands of dollars, weeks of time, and countless headaches. Employees are an expensive component in any firm, and employers want to make certain they are hiring the best workers money can buy.

The interview is not just a formality designed to make sure you don't have two heads or a set of horns. It is the important final stage in a process through which companies and institutions fill their offices and factories with the best people available. Consequently, employers take interviews very seriously. And so should you.

From your perspective, an interview can be a grand opportunity to show an employer why you should be hired. Try to think of your interview not as one more barrier you must overcome but rather as an adventure and a challenge. You will probably have 30 to 60 minutes alone with someone who has the authority to give you what you want—a better job and probably a better future.

If you'd like an image to tuck away in the back of your mind, think of your interview as a door leading to the job or career you desire. Now, if you conceive of that door as locked or jammed shut or bolted or blocked from the other side, you aren't likely ever to get through. But if you perceive that door as one that only needs to be opened and passed through, you'll have no trouble.

## The Medium Is the Message

Your resume was simply a vehicle for getting information to an employer. It had no intrinsic value of its own. Your interview will be different. If a company were only interested in obtaining answers to specific questions, it could just as well send you a list and have you respond in writing. But an interview is much more than a series of questions and answers. Everything about you, from your haircut to your grammar to your attitude, will be taken into account in an interview. THE MESSAGE IS YOU.

## Kinds of Interviews

Most often, an employment interview consists of one person—the owner, personnel director, recruiter, or someone else from the firm—talking with you one-on-one in an office setting. It will be a private affair in comfortable surroundings and usually will be uninterrupted by phone calls and intruders. Frequently, you may meet this way with a second or third person in the firm—perhaps a division manager or foreman. The interview may be as brief as 30 minutes, or rarely it may last all day.

Another interview form you may encounter is the panel interview, in which you may meet with three or four members of the firm at one time. In terms of your conduct, the only difference here is that you now have three or four names to learn, remember and use, and there are three or four sets of eyes with which you must maintain contact (more about names and eye contact later).

Sometimes, a candidate (usually only at the management level) is invited to be interviewed over lunch. If you are invited to a lunch interview, keep the following items in mind: (1) Order the same general type of food as your interviewer. If he/she is eating soup and sandwich, you should not order the prime rib. (2) Avoid food that is messy to eat and/or difficult to handle. You probably aren't going to conduct a good interview while slurping spaghetti or chomping on corn-on-the-cob. (3) You probably will be better off if you refrain from all alcoholic drinks. You don't want to impair your mental processes even in the slightest. Order a soft drink, milk, or coffee instead. (4) Remember throughout the lunch that you are being interviewed. The informal setting may entice you to see this as a social function rather than as business, but your interviewer will be continually evaluating you.

There's one more kind of interview you should be aware of, even though you will likely never encounter it. At one time and at certain employment levels, employers conducted stress interviews with job candidates. The main purpose of the interview was to put the applicant under stress and observe his/her reactions. One tactic was to offer an interviewee a cigarette when no ashtrays were available. In another ploy, the candidate would be escorted by a secretary into the interviewer's office and left standing before his/her desk. The interviewer, pretending to be oblivious to the job seeker's presence, would continue writing or shuffling papers as the minutes ticked by. Another tactic was to disagree with everything an applicant said in an interview. If the candidate said the weather was beautiful, the interviewer complained of the heat, and so on. Supposedly, employers could learn important things about an applicant by the way he/she reacted in these stress situations. Fortunately, the stress interview is almost extinct in most normal employment situations.

# Preparation

Employment counselors continually report that the most common interview mistake made by job applicants is failure to prepare properly. It is not enough simply to get a good night's sleep and assume you'll make your best impression in an interview. Getting ready for an interview requires work, research, and practice.

You will be expected to know something about the firm or institution with which you'll be interviewing. How large is it? When was it founded? What are its major products or services? How diversified is it? Does it own any other companies? Where are its main branches? What is its business philosophy? What major internal changes have taken place recently? In what capacity does this firm use people with your skills? In short, become as familiar with the firm as you can. Your interviewer will expect nothing less. Also, you should be aware of recent trends and happenings within the industry as a whole.

One way to learn about the company is to visit it. If public tours are available, take one. If not, visit the firm's public relations office and ask for any printed material—brochures, pamphlets, copies of articles, reports, clippings—about the company. One specific document that can tell you a lot about the firm is its last annual report. Get a copy. There's no need to disguise your motives. In fact, your curiosity would probably be admired by the boss if he were to learn of it.

Another source of information is the library. Several books are available to give you a thumbnail sketch of the firm, its leaders, financial standing, and other information. Simply ask a reference librarian to direct you to possible sources. If the firm is a major one, magazine and newspaper articles may have been written about it. Check the *New York Times Index*, *Wall Street Journal Index*, and *Reader's Guide to Periodical Literature*. Some libraries also keep on file copies of corporate annual reports.

If there is a college, university, or vocational school in your area, visit its placement office. Most such institutions maintain a library of material about firms to which its students frequently apply.

One other possible source of information is the brokers who buy and sell that firm's stock. Look in your phone book's yellow pages under "stock brokers" and give a few of them a call. It's their job to know about the companies they deal with, and they may be able to pass that information on to you.

# Practice

Don't rely on your spontaneity to carry you favorably through the interview. Under the stress of an interview, completely normal people have had their minds go blank, forgotten their employer's name, and couldn't remember if they were married. Usually this sort of thing happens because the interviewee did not practice for the interview. He/she went in cold, and the pressure of the moment made a blithering idiot out of an otherwise capable person.

The best way to begin practicing is to anticipate the questions you might be asked. Many questions are standard interview fare regardless of your profession. Write down or at least rehearse in your mind how you might answer each of them. Here are some of the questions interviewers most often ask (three of these will be discussed in more detail later):

- Tell me something about yourself.
- What do you see yourself doing five years from now?
- What are your long-range career goals?
- Why did you enter your field of work?
- Why do you want to work for our company?
- How do you think other people would describe you?
- What are your greatest strengths and weaknesses?
- Why should we hire you?
- What are your greatest accomplishments?
- How well do you work under pressure?
- Name one problem you've encountered on the job and tell how you solved it.
- What have you learned on your present (last) job?
- Why do you want to quit your present job? (Or, why did you quit your last job?)
- Are you a leader or a follower?
- Are you a competitive person?

- How do you feel about a job requiring relocation and travel?
- What salary will you require?
- What do you do in your spare time?
- How do you get along with the people you work for and with?

Compose concise, clear, informative answers to these questions and to any others you think may be asked. With a stop watch, practice responding to them out loud. If you're taking much more than a minute on any of them, you're probably running on too long. Often 30 seconds will be sufficient. If you're hearing the question for the first time in the interview, however, it may take you that long just to organize your thoughts, and 30 seconds of silence during an interview seems like an eternity. So, get your thoughts organized before the interview. But, you should not attempt to memorize a response. That will sound phony, and you may run into trouble if you lose your place in your little speech. Simply have an outline of a response firmly in mind.

Besides anticipating questions and answers, one of the most valuable things you can do to get ready for an interview is to conduct a skills inventory. What can you do? What do you have to offer an employer? What personality characteristics make you an attractive candidate for the job? Are you loyal, conscientious, hard-working, dependable, able to accept responsibility, creative, caring, thorough, and outgoing? Do you finish every project you start? Do you take orders well? Do you give orders well? Can you work without a lot of supervision? Do you ask questions when you don't understand something? Do you like challenges in the form of problems that need solving? What is there about you that should make an employer want to hire you?

Take a piece of paper and actually make a list of these qualities. Try to think of a specific example from your past that illustrates each. Study this inventory until you have at the tip of your tongue a wealth of positive information about yourself. Now, think about these skills and abilities in terms of some of the questions you are likely to be asked. When an interviewer asks you to say something about yourself or explain why you should be hired or discuss your strengths, work several of these skills and abilities into your answer.

Once you feel prepared to deliver good answers to the questions, recruit a friend to assist you in a dress rehearsal. Let your acquaintance play the part of the interviewer by asking you the questions. Answer them just as you hope to do in the interview—that is, in complete, well-planned sentences. Be specific and be brief. Going through such a mock interview can do wonders for the quality of your answers, and it will likely reduce your nervousness when the real interview begins.

And you may want to tape record the practice sessions to evaluate the quality of your voice and the number of times you slip expressions like "yeah," "you know," "uh huh," and "umm" into the conversation. If your voice comes out in a monotone, make an extra effort to inject enthusiasm into it. You are, in a very real sense, a performer, and you will be judged on HOW you say something as well as on WHAT you say. If you have access to a video recorder, put your practice interviews on tape and later critique everything from your posture to your haircut (more about those later).

# Asking the Asker

Another important part of getting ready for an interview is to prepare questions that you will ask the interviewer. In many interviews, the most awkward moment comes when the applicant is asked, "Do you have any questions about our company or about this job?" Too often, the interviewee is taken by surprise and mumbles something like, "No, not really." An interviewer is likely to interpret this lack of questions as indifference toward the firm, and most employers are looking for people with a keen interest in their companies. So, be prepared with several good questions about the company. If you want, you may even jot these down on note cards that you'll have handy during the interview.

These questions should not revolve around the fringe benefits you may be wondering about. Don't ask about vacations, holidays, sick leave, health insurance, or other perquisites. Center your questions on the job for which you're being considered and on the needs of the company. Use this opportunity not to satisfy your curiosity but to impress the interviewer with your interest in the firm. Most of these questions will relate only to the firm and job involved, but the following examples may give you an idea of the kind you might want to ask:

- Why is this position currently open?
- How is this department organized?
- What is the first major problem you'll want me to tackle?
- What are the strengths and weaknesses of the department (or office or shop) in which I'll be working?
- Exactly what qualities are you looking for in the person who will fill the position?
- Does the company have plans for expansion or new products?
- How will the computer revolution (or recent legislation or some other new factor) affect the firm?
- What is the relationship between the firm and its competitors?

# Get There on Time

Now that you are fully prepared to be interviewed, a myriad of details must be attended to. Foremost among these is getting yourself to the interview location on time. Unless you are intimately familiar with the route, traffic patterns, and location of the building, you should allot at least half an hour for minor emergencies such as wrong turns. Even if you know exactly how to get there, it's always good to have enough extra time so that you can change a flat tire or detour around unexpected road construction. If all goes well and you arrive at your destination 30 minutes early, you can collect your thoughts over a cup of coffee in a nearby restaurant.

If the unthinkable happens and you see that you are going to be unavoidably late, find a phone and call your interviewer. Your appointment may simply be moved back, or you may be rescheduled for another day. If you don't call but rather come bursting into the office 15 minutes late, you'll be making a negative first impression that may be extremely difficult to overcome.

Plan to enter the firm's office five or ten minutes before your appointment time. Getting there any earlier is in poor taste, and cutting it much closer than that may indicate to the interviewer that you either don't plan your time well or aren't really serious about this job. Use the few minutes before your interview starts to observe the office surroundings, chat with a secretary, relax, or go over once more in your mind the main points you want to get across in the interview.

# You Can't Take It With You

Just about everything you'll need for a successful interview must be transported in your head. Don't take a briefcase full of impressive documents (transcripts, letters of reference, etc.) to the interview unless you've been asked to do so. You should, however, take one or two extra copies of your resume, as there may be more than one person at the company who needs to have one. Also, you may want to have a pen and small notebook handy during the interview so you can jot down a question you'd like to ask but had not anticipated. Don't take with you any material relating to other interviews you have scheduled or any printed matter relating to the firm you're visiting. You won't impress an interviewer by walking in with a copy of the company's last annual report under your arm.

And under no circumstances should you take another person with you to the interview. Some teenagers feel more secure if a friend tags along to an interview, but this buddy system definitely portrays you as immature and childish. If you have to drop your spouse off at work after the interview, have him/her wait in the car or in a nearby coffee shop. Interviews must be flown solo.

# Looking Like a Winner

Unless you're applying for a job at the *Avant Garde Monthly*, there is only one way to dress for an interview: CONSERVATIVELY. The business world is not at all interested in how creatively you can attire yourself. You should not wear flamboyant, sporty clothing to any interview, no matter how good it may make you look or how popular the style is at your favorite discotheque. Nor should you wear whatever you happen to have worn the day before.

Every occupation and profession has a "uniform" of some sort, and you probably will be expected to wear that uniform to your interviews. The "uniform" may be a three-piece suit for a sales representative or blouse and skirt for a teacher or slacks and shirt for a store clerk.

Here are a few guidelines to help you decide what to wear to your interview (not all of them will apply to every occupation): (1) Dress as though you were arriving for your first day on the job. This might apply to teachers, accountants, secretaries, clerks, receptionists, and the like. However, if you're applying for a job such as a mechanic, nurse, policeman, or fireman, you obviously should not wear your "working clothes" to your interview. (2) Dress just a bit better than you think regular workers at this firm do. (3) Wear what you expect the interviewer might wear. This may vary from a coat and tie to work pants and shirt. (4) If you are truly in doubt about duds, wear a suit or sport coat with tie (men) or a dress (women). Always keep the apparel conservative; the only guidelines that apply to everyone are to show up for your interview wearing clothes that are clean, neat, and wrinkle-free.

A few additional clothing tips are in order. Carry keys and wallet in a jacket or purse rather than in a pants pocket so unsightly bulges are avoided. Women can avoid the appearance of having dressed too sexily by keeping their necklines high, their hemlines low, and their slacks not overly tight. Men should wear over-the-calf socks so skin doesn't show when they cross their legs. Neckties should not be of the clip-on variety. Keep jewelry to a minimum.

Your personal hygiene and grooming must be impeccable too. Here's a list of reminders:

- A man's hair should be conservatively cut. A woman's hairdo should be attractive but not flamboyant. Clean, combed hair is always a must.
- Some employers seem to dislike beards, so a man's job chances are better if he's clean-shaven. Moustaches usually are okay, however.
- Dirt under fingernails is taboo, even if the job opening is for a farmer.
- If it's been a while since your teeth have been cleaned by a dental hygienist, maybe now is the time.
- If you're worried about bad breath, use a breath mint. Never chew gum during an interview.
- Clip nasal hairs if they're unsightly.
- Women should use special discretion in applying makeup. Don't pour it on just because the interview is important.
- Shower or bathe not long before the interview.
- Perfumes and colognes should be used very sparingly. Or better yet, don't use them at all.

# Talking Without Words

Intentionally or not, some interviewers make up their minds about applicants even before the candidate has opened his/her mouth. Everything you've ever heard about the importance of first impressions is true. The first minute with an interviewer is the most important of all, and even during the interview, your actions may speak more loudly than your words. It's called body language, and you are "talking" a mile a minute even though your lips may be closed.

Your first body language "utterance" may be in the form of a handshake. Nothing so destroys a good first impression as a limp, dead-fish handshake. A handshake that lacks strength and firmness labels you as being weak, indecisive, and short on confidence. If your handshake has all the vigor of yesterday's spaghetti, an interviewer may wonder how you'll ever be able to close a sale, discipline a worker, or handle a customer's complaint. Make your shake solid and strong.

You're going to be nervous and your palms may be perspiring, so try your best to keep your right hand dry. If the interviewer offers his/her hand, grip it firmly, make a couple of quick pumps, and let go. If no hand is offered, don't worry about it. Handshaking just may not be part of the interviewer's style.

Smile at the interviewer as you greet each other. It's always easier to like people who are friendly, so try to project an amiable image. Flash a quick, honest smile that tells the interviewer you're a pleasant person to be around.

Probably the most important bit of body language you can use is to LOOK THE INTERVIEWER IN THE EYE. Establish eye contact with your interviewer as you meet each other and maintain that connection throughout the interview. Regular eye contact proclaims your confidence, honesty, and extroverted nature. Constantly looking away from a person marks you as shy, uncertain of yourself, weak, and indecisive.

This does not mean that you must stare like a zombie at your questioner during the entire interview. It is normal for conversationalists to break eye contact regularly, but your gaze should always return to the other person's eyes. Usually, this will work best if you look at the other person's eyes while he/she is speaking to you and then break eye contact briefly as you think about a response and begin to speak. Sometime during your answer, however, your eyes should again meet the interviewer's. Don't talk to the floor or the ceiling. If you're being interviewed by more than one person, try to share your eye contact equally among them.

While you're going through mock interviews with a friend, practice eye contact. Practice it too with store clerks, secretaries, mailmen, and any other people you meet. After a few sessions of forcing yourself to look directly into strangers' eyes, you'll become comfortable with it and will have acquired a valuable social asset.

Another important body language message comes from your posture. A slouch says you're weak and ineffectual. Leaning forward onto the interviewer's desk may mark you as someone who is brazen and overly aggressive. Sit and stand erect with your back perfectly straight. If you want to cross your legs, do so at the knees, not the ankles. Try to find a comfortable position and keep it. Don't fidget and change position every couple of minutes. Proper posture can aid you in coming across as an alert, confident individual.

Everyone is somewhat nervous during interviews, and often that affliction shows up in an interviewee's hands. Plan to find something for your hands to do. Keep them folded together in your lap. Hold on to the small notebook you may be carrying. If you're sitting at a table, you may be better off placing your hands out of sight beneath it. If you can lace your fingers together and keep them that way without twiddling your thumbs or picking at your fingernails, then it's okay to keep them in view.

Resolve to keep your hands away from your hair and face during the interview. You may have to work hard to achieve this, as the temptation may be overwhelming to pat your hair into shape, stroke your chin, rub your nose, or adjust your glasses.

If you suffer from minor nervous tics, such as excessive blinking, nodding, stumbling over your words, scratching or running your fingers through your hair, work especially hard in practice to maintain an appearance free of these distracting habits.

# Interview Etiquette

Your interviewer will be observing how you conduct yourself. Be on your best behavior and don't give anyone any reason to doubt that you are a courteous, thoughtful, socially competent person. Here are a few general rules to follow:

- If you're going to be late for an interview, or if you must cancel altogether, call as soon as possible. Everyone values time, and you're going to make an enemy if you fail to let the interviewer know as soon as possible that there must be a change in plan.
- Wait to be seated. Remain standing until the interviewer asks you to sit or gestures toward a chair. This is the interviewer's show, so let him/her run it.
- Let the interviewer begin the conversation. If he/she wants to engage in small talk for a minute or so, go along with it. Don't launch uninvited into a recitation of your strong points.
- Don't interrupt the interviewer. Let him/her completely finish a question before you begin to respond.
- Don't smoke. Even if the interviewer is puffing away and you won't be offending anyone, forego the cigarettes. The last thing you need is to drop hot ashes in your lap.
- Don't criticize former employers. Almost any disparaging remarks you make about past bosses can be interpreted as "sour grapes" on your part, especially

if you were fired from the job. Also, the interviewer may wonder what bad words you'll eventually have to say about him/her.

- As the interview draws to a close, make sure you know what the next step will be. Should you call back in a few days? Will the firm contact you regardless of its choice? Will there be another interview for the finalists?
- Recognize when the interview is over. When the interviewer thanks you for coming, promises to get in touch with you, rises from his/her chair, or in some other way indicates that your interview has ended, you should make a quick and graceful exit.
- Send a thank-you note to the firm a day or so after the interview. See Chapter 5 for guidelines on writing such a letter.

# Getting Your Message Across

People get nervous during interviews because they know strangers will be evaluating them based on only 30 minutes of conversation and observation. Many job seekers go to an interview with the idea that the best approach is simply to avoid making a mistake. They believe that if they don't "blow" an interview, they have succeeded. Consequently, they're afraid to actively sell themselves. They answer the questions, but that's about all.

A much better approach is to look upon the interview as an adventure. A challenge. If you don't get hired, you will be exactly where you were before the interview. Nothing that was yours in the first place will have been lost. Take your best shot at selling yourself. Don't just sit there waiting to be discovered.

You should actively attempt to show the interviewer that you are the kind of person his/her firm needs. Treat the interviewer and other people in the office with courtesy and respect. Be cooperative in scheduling, providing materials, and all other matters. Display enthusiasm for the job and interest in the firm. Concentrate on avoiding displays of negativism, conceit, greed, indifference, verbosity, and high-pressure selling.

Be honest in all your dealings with the firm and the interviewer. Never tell your questioner what you think he/she wants to hear if it is not the truth. Many interviewers are veterans at their job and can spot a phony two blocks away. Besides, your lies will likely return to haunt you, perhaps even before the interview is over.

Listen carefully to an entire question before you begin to respond. An applicant who begins formulating an answer in his/her mind while the interviewer is still speaking will likely miss part of the question. And listen carefully to what is being asked. It may be different from the question you had anticipated.

Show that you have a sense of humor. Don't plan on telling jokes during your interview, but do be prepared to laugh if something humorous occurs. Some interviewers prefer to punctuate the conversation with light moments. Go along with that style when you encounter it. Show that you are a well-rounded individual who is easy to get along with.

Perhaps the quality you should strive hardest to display is confidence. Competence alone may not be enough. Employers often are looking for people who know they are good at what they do. Without being cocky or boastful, let the interviewer know that you do your job well. Let him/her know that you are proud of what you have done and of what you can do. One simple trick that will help you feel and act confident is to memorize the interviewer's name the first time you hear it and then use it a few times during the conversation. In general, you should enter an interview with the same pride and confidence you would have if you were an automobile salesperson and had just sold a fleet of luxury cars.

Go beyond simple answers to the questions. Have prepared in your mind the details of your past successes and use these stories to illustrate your good qualities. Be specific and give plenty of facts. Speak in facts ("I cut shoplifting 50 percent in my former employer's store.") and not in opinions. ("I was instrumental in reducing shoplifting in my former employer's store.") Either before or during the interview, try to determine which of the firm's needs you might be able to fulfill. Then explain to the interviewer exactly how you will be able to help the company.

When you are asked to mention some of your strong points, speak in terms of the way you accept responsibility, your resourcefulness, ingenuity, loyalty, or other overall qualities. Don't say that your greatest strength is that you can type 75 words per minute or lift 200 pounds.

SAY IT WITH GRACE. Practice making your points in an articulate manner. Speak in complete sentences. Use the best grammar and usage and vocabulary you have at your command. Try to eliminate from your speech the phrases "you know," "ya," "uh huh," "umm," and the like. Project your voice in strong tones. Avoid a monotone. Use expression in your speech. And stop as soon as you have made your point. Don't let your sentences trail off to an ineffective conclusion.

# Three Tough Questions

Thorough preparation should put you in good shape for answering most questions posed by the interviewer. There are, however, three questions that deserve a bit of extra thought and consideration if you are to answer them in the best possible manner.

### — What are some of your strengths and weaknesses? —

You should be able to describe your strengths without much trouble. This question, in fact, provides a wide-open opportunity for you to talk about virtually any positive aspects of your background and personality.

The potential problem for most people lies in discussing their weaknesses. Baring your soul and stating your shortcomings in blatantly negative terms is the WRONG thing to do. You may score a point for candor, but you won't move any closer to getting the job. Even though the interviewer asks about your weaknesses, he/she doesn't really expect you to say grossly negative things about yourself.

Let's say one of your weaknesses is that you have a lot of trouble delegating authority. Don't respond by saying, "I am lousy at delegating authority," or "I'm not very comfortable in assigning work to other people." Try to find some way to present this weakness as something of an asset. You might say, "I am such a perfectionist that I often end up doing jobs myself that probably should be delegated to others." Or, "I sometimes prefer to do a job myself when it really should be assigned to someone else." With the latter responses, you come across sounding like a perfectionist and hard worker instead of like an ineffectual manager.

Another example. If you sometimes make mistakes on the job because you fail to "go by the book," you may be tempted to respond like this: "I sometimes have trouble following accepted procedures." Or "I guess I don't always follow the shop guidelines." You can, however, turn this liability into an asset with responses like this: "I like to be creative in the way I solve problems, but not all my ideas work." Or, "I like to come up with new and better ways of doing things, and sometimes I end up straying away from shop guidelines." The last two responses make you sound creative, not slipshod. Think about your weaknesses. You can probably present them in equally positive terms.

### — Why did you quit your last job? —

This question also may be asked about your present job or about any one out of your past. The temptation is to blame your former employer: "It was a dead-end job." Or, "I never got the promotions I deserved." Or, "There was too much office politics." Or, "My supervisor was impossible to work for." Try to resist these jabs at former employers, as they only serve to make you sound spiteful, resentful, and heavy with grudges.

Instead, present your reasons for leaving in positive terms, possibly referring to the company with which you are now interviewing. You should try, however, to avoid direct comparisons between past employers and your potential new one. Here are some possibilities: "I'm looking for a job that has a lot of career potential." Or, "I knew I was worth more money than they could afford to pay me." Or, "I prefer the organizational structure of a firm like yours."

### — What salary will you need? —

Somewhere near the end of the interview, or possibly later in a follow-up interview, the talk necessarily will turn to salary. You should have a couple of figures firmly in your mind. First, you should know your absolute bottom line, below which you will turn down the job. That absolute minimum will depend greatly on your personal circumstances. But for every person and every job, there is some salary figure that represents too little pay for too much work. The first figure is relatively easy to determine. How much are you worth? How much money do you need to live? Each of us has our own answers to those questions.

Second, you should have ready a salary figure (or salary range) you intend to ask for. This is how much you WANT, not how much you NEED. Many employment counselors suggest you arrive at this figure by increasing your present (or last) salary by 20 percent. If you're making $30,000 on your present job, you may want to ask for $36,000 as a starting salary on your new job. The desire for a higher salary is a factor in nearly all changes of employment, and, other circumstances being equal, potential employers will expect to pay you more than did your previous employer.

"I need $36,000." A flat statement such as this may backfire on you because it sounds like a take-it-or-leave-it offer. If the company says it can pay only $35,000, you've backed yourself into a corner. A better idea is to offer a range of acceptable salaries. One way to do this is to start just below the salary you'd like and extend the range a few thousand dollars beyond. If you would like $36,000, would be overjoyed at $40,000, but would settle for $35,000, a good range to suggest might be $35,000 to $40,000. This way, you have some room to negotiate. And remember to consider fringe benefits (insurance coverage, vacations, stock options) when computing your desired and acceptable salaries.

One final point on salary. Most entry-level and many other jobs do not have much negotiating room built into the salary structure. In other words, it may be a buyer's market in which the employer sets the salary, and you either must take it or leave it. If you are applying for such jobs, you should try to find out before your interview approximately how much pay is being offered. Then, if that amount is acceptable, you can respond with a similar figure if your interviewer asks about your salary needs. You usually can learn the salary range being offered by checking a formal job listing or advertisement or by calling the employer's office.

# Getting Ready to Do It Again

As soon as you get home after your interview, critically examine your performance. Did you exude confidence? Did you talk too much? Too little? Did you stumble on certain questions? Did you answer some questions poorly? Were you too nervous? Did you continually fuss with your papers? Did you smile? Did you shake hands firmly? And so on. Practice improving the weak aspects of your interviewing technique. Take pride in your strong points. Get ready for your next interview. If you don't get this job, you just may land an even better one the next time out. Good luck.

# ARCO Books to Improve your Office Skills

## BRUSHING UP YOUR CLERICAL SKILLS
**Eve P. Steinberg.** Practice exercises to bring back typing speed and accuracy. Drills to improve filing efficiency. Dictation practice to shore up stenographic skills. Ideal for anyone seeking a first office job or a return to office work after a long absence.
ISBN 0-668-05538-3 Paper **$5.95**

## WORD PROCESSING SIMPLIFIED AND SELF-TAUGHT
**Jane Christensen.** Introduction to how word processing systems operate. Explanations of all word processing applications. Analysis of all hardware.
ISBN 0-668-05601-0 Paper **$4.95**

## THE SECRETARY'S QUICK REFERENCE HANDBOOK
**Sheryl L. Lindsell.** Concise guide to the basics of business English, the fundamentals of business letter writing and the essentials of office practice and procedure.
ISBN 0-668-05595-2 Paper **$3.95**

## TYPING FOR EVERYONE
**Nathan Levine.** A quick and expert way to learn touch typing. Thirty-five easy lessons with timed-typing score sheets.
ISBN 0-668-04975-8 Easel-back **$6.95**

## TEACH YOURSELF TYPING
**Nathan Levine.** A brief self-teaching guide to touch typing. Thirty short lessons lead to maximum proficiency in a minimum amount of time.
ISBN 0-668-05455-7 Paper **$3.95**

## QUICKSCRIPT: THE FAST AND SIMPLE SHORTHAND METHOD
**Adele Booth Blanchard.** Complete instruction and numerous practice exercises for mastering the quickscript shorthand method.
ISBN 0-668-05572-3 Paper **$5.95**

*For book ordering information refer to the last page of this book.*

**ORDER THE BOOKS DESCRIBED ON THE PREVIOUS PAGES FROM YOUR
BOOKSELLER OR DIRECTLY FROM:**

**PRENTICE HALL PRESS**
c/o SIMON & SCHUSTER MAIL ORDER BILLING
Route 59 at Brook Hill Drive
West Nyack, NY 10994

To order directly, complete the coupon below. Enclose a check or money order for the total amount or include credit card information. No C.O.D.s accepted.

To order by phone, call 201-767-5937.

*MAIL THIS COUPON TODAY!*

Mail to: **Prentice Hall Press, c/o Simon & Schuster Mail Order Billing,
Route 59 at Brook Hill Drive, West Nyack, NY 10994.**
*Please rush the following books:*

| NO. OF COPIES | TITLE # | TITLE | UNIT PRICE | TOTAL |
|---|---|---|---|---|
| | | | | |
| | | | | |
| | | | | |
| | | | | |
| | | | | |
| | | | | |
| | | | | |
| | | | SUB-TOTAL | |
| | | | SALES TAX FOR YOUR STATE | |
| | | | 12% PACKING & MAILING | |
| | | | TOTAL | |

I enclose check ☐, M.O. ☐, for $_____ or charge my ☐ VISA ☐ MASTERCARD

Account # _____ Exp. Date _____

Signature _____

NAME _____

ADDRESS _____

CITY _____ STATE _____ ZIP _____

*Every Arco book is guaranteed. Return for full refund within ten days
if not completely satisfied.*

**NOT RESPONSIBLE FOR CASH SENT THROUGH THE MAILS**